CHINESE LOVE SIGNS

USING THE SECRETS OF THE ANCIENT
CHINESE ZODIAC TO FIND TRUE LOVE

L.A. JUSTICE

ADAMS MEDIA CORPORATION
Avon, Massachusetts

This book is dedicated to anyone who is looking for love;
and to my daughter, Ananda, who let me use
the computer even when her term papers were due!

Published by
Adams Media Corporation
57 Littlefield Street, Avon MA 02322. U.S.A.
www.adamsmedia.com

ISBN: 1-58062-853-2

Printed in Canada.

J I H G F E D C B A

Library of Congress Cataloging-in-Publication Data
Justice, L.A.
Chinese love signs / by L.A. Justice.
p.   cm.
ISBN 1-58062-853-2
1. Astrology, Chinese. 2. Love—Miscellanea. I. Title.
BF1714.C5 J87 2003
133.5'9251—dc21
2002011338

This publication is designed to provide accurate and authoritative information with
regard to the subject matter covered. It is sold with the understanding that the pub-
lisher is not engaged in rendering legal, accounting, or other professional advice. If
legal advice or other expert assistance is required, the services of a competent professional person should be sought.
    —From a *Declaration of Principles* jointly adopted by a Committee of the
American Bar Association and a Committee of Publishers and Associations

Many of the designations used by manufacturers and sellers to distinguish their
products are claimed as trademarks. Where those designations appear in this
book and Adams Media was aware of a trademark claim, the designations have
been printed with initial capital letters.

Cover illustrations and interior zodiac art by Roberta Collier-Morales.

This book is available at quantity discounts for bulk purchases.
For information, call 1-800-872-5627.

Table of Contents

Acknowledgments

My heartfelt thanks to Sophie Cathro, Kate McBride, Danielle Chiotti, Laura MacLaughlin, and Claire Gerus at Adams Media Corporation. Without their able assistance, this book would not be in print. And a special note of appreciation to Khrysti Nazzaro for her right-on-the-money suggestions.

Another round of applause for my dear friend Julie Williams, who provided her insights on sun signs and how they affect us.

INTRODUCTION

The Origin of the Chinese Zodiac

Since ancient times, people throughout the world have believed that the time of one's birth determined one's destiny.

For centuries, people in the East have consulted philosophers and seers to determine an "auspicious" day for such major events as engagements, weddings, burials, moving, and business deals. The Chinese zodiac is so significant that some Asian women have even taken medication to delay the birth of a child so that the infant would be born on a more meaningful day, when the stars and planets are in better alignment.

Both Eastern and Western civilizations have developed methods by which your personality can be understood and defined in relation to animal attributes. In the West, your sign is based on the month in which you were born; the signs include the lion, the crab, and even the dual personality of twins—or the sign of Gemini. In the East, the symbol of your animal nature is predetermined by the year in which you were born; the signs include the Rat, the Ox, the Tiger, and the Pig.

According to the Chinese zodiac, the "animal nature" that governs the year of your birth can help you figure out your own fundamental nature—or why you act the way you do in certain situations. If you were born in the year of the Rooster, you may be picky; and if you were born in the year of the Ox, chances are you may move at a slower pace than someone born in the years of the Monkey or the Dragon. These clues to your personality are very important in order to understand yourself and others in terms of compatibility both in love and in day-to-day interaction.

The relationship between the Chinese zodiac and love is so strong that parents often consult an astrologer about prospective spouses for their children. If the family feels that a Rooster male is not well matched to their Rat daughter, they will call off the marriage. No matter how lovers come together, their signs will exert a powerful influence. The basic personality traits that are the product of our "animal nature" can be used to evaluate who will make the best business partner, lover, and friend. That's what this book is all about.

Once you are aware of your qualities—both the good traits and those that need improving—you can work on developing your pleasant qualities while eliminating those that are less appealing. With the self-knowledge you gain from the Chinese zodiac, you can mold your life to be richer and fuller so you can get exactly what you want—including the partner of your dreams.

By using the handy "For Better or Worse" synopses in each chapter, you will have a bird's-eye view of how you will interact with others. Certain signs naturally get along, others are so-so combinations requiring a little more work to make it a smooth ride. Some signs just don't mix well at all, which explains why some people "rub you the wrong way." As you review each of these pairings, you can see why some relationships are easy and others are filled with problems.

Finally, at the end of each chapter, you can read about a celebrity couple and see how their Chinese zodiac works—and how it can work for you.

FINDING YOUR SIGN

The Chinese calendar is based on the movement of the Moon, so the beginning of the year doesn't always start on the first of the month. Listed below are the exact dates for each sign, as well as the corresponding element. To find your sign, look up the day, month, and year you were born. Remember, the Chinese horoscope is based on twelve-year cycles.

Feb. 5, 1924 to Jan. 24, 1925	Rat
Jan. 25, 1925 to Feb. 12, 1926	Ox
Feb. 13, 1926 to Feb. 1, 1927	Tiger
Feb. 2, 1927 to Jan. 22, 1928	Rabbit
Jan. 23, 1928 to Feb. 9, 1929	Dragon
Feb. 10, 1929 to Jan. 29, 1930	Snake
Jan. 30, 1930 to Feb. 16, 1931	Horse
Feb. 17, 1931 to Feb. 5, 1932	Sheep
Feb. 6, 1932 to Jan. 25, 1933	Monkey
Jan. 26, 1933 to Feb. 13, 1934	Rooster

Feb. 14, 1934 to Feb. 3, 1935	Dog
Feb. 4, 1935 to Jan. 23, 1936	Pig
Jan. 24, 1936 to Feb. 10, 1937	Rat
Feb. 11, 1937 to Jan. 30, 1938	Ox
Jan. 31, 1938 to Feb. 18, 1939	Tiger
Feb. 19, 1939 to Feb. 7, 1940	Rabbit
Feb. 8, 1940 to Jan. 26, 1941	Dragon
Jan. 27, 1941 to Feb. 14, 1942	Snake
Feb. 15, 1942 to Feb. 4, 1943	Horse
Feb. 5, 1943 to Jan. 24, 1944	Sheep
Jan. 25, 1944 to Feb. 12, 1945	Monkey
Feb. 13, 1945 to Feb. 1, 1946	Rooster
Feb. 2, 1946 to Jan. 21, 1947	Dog
Jan. 22, 1947 to Feb. 9, 1948	Pig
Feb. 10, 1948 to Jan. 28, 1949	Rat
Jan. 29, 1949 to Feb. 16, 1950	Ox
Feb. 17, 1950 to Feb. 5, 1951	Tiger
Feb. 6, 1951 to Jan. 26, 1952	Rabbit
Jan. 27, 1952 to Feb. 13, 1953	Dragon
Feb. 14, 1953 to Feb. 2, 1954	Snake
Feb. 3, 1954 to Jan. 23, 1955	Horse
Jan. 24, 1955 to Feb. 11, 1956	Sheep
Feb. 12, 1956 to Jan. 30, 1957	Monkey
Jan. 31, 1957 to Feb. 17, 1958	Rooster
Feb. 18, 1958 to Feb. 7, 1959	Dog
Feb. 8, 1959 to Jan. 27, 1960	Pig
Jan. 28, 1960 to Feb. 14, 1961	Rat
Feb. 15, 1961 to Feb. 4, 1962	Ox

Feb. 5, 1962 to Jan. 24, 1963	Tiger
Jan. 25, 1963 to Feb. 12, 1964	Rabbit
Feb. 13 1964 to Feb. 1, 1965	Dragon
Feb. 2, 1965 to Jan. 20, 1966	Snake
Jan. 21, 1966 to Feb. 8, 1967	Horse
Feb. 9, 1967 to Jan. 29, 1968	Sheep
Jan. 30, 1968 to Feb. 16, 1969	Monkey
Feb. 17, 1969 to Feb. 5, 1970	Rooster
Feb. 6, 1970 to Jan. 26, 1971	Dog
Jan. 27, 1971 to Jan. 15, 1972	Pig
Jan. 16, 1972 to Feb. 2, 1973	Rat
Feb. 3, 1973 to Jan. 22, 1974	Ox
Jan. 23, 1974 to Feb. 10, 1975	Tiger
Feb. 11, 1975 to Jan. 30, 1976	Rabbit
Jan. 31, 1976 to Feb. 17, 1977	Dragon
Feb. 18, 1977 to Feb. 6, 1978	Snake
Feb. 7, 1978 to Jan. 27, 1979	Horse
Jan. 28, 1979 to Feb. 15, 1980	Sheep
Feb. 16, 1980 to Feb. 4, 1981	Monkey
Feb. 5, 1981 to Jan. 24, 1982	Rooster
Jan. 25, 1982 to Feb. 12, 1983	Dog
Feb. 13, 1983 to Feb. 1, 1984	Pig
Feb. 2, 1984 to Feb. 19, 1985	Rat
Feb. 20, 1985 to Feb. 8, 1986	Ox
Feb. 9, 1986 to Jan. 28, 1987	Tiger
Jan. 29, 1987 to Feb. 16, 1988	Rabbit
Feb. 17, 1988 to Feb. 5, 1989	Dragon
Feb. 6, 1989 to Jan. 26, 1990	Snake

Jan. 27, 1990 to Feb. 14, 1991	Horse
Feb. 15, 1991 to Feb. 3, 1992	Sheep
Feb. 4, 1992 to Jan. 22, 1993	Monkey
Jan. 23, 1993 to Feb. 9, 1994	Rooster
Feb. 10, 1994 to Jan. 30, 1995	Dog
Jan. 31, 1995 to Feb. 18, 1996	Pig

The Romantic Rat

Years of the Rat: 1900, 1912, 1924, 1936, 1948, 1960, 1972, 1984, and 1996

Famous Rats: Wolfgang Amadeus Mozart, Clark Gable, Cameron Diaz, Marlon Brando, and Ben Affleck

Season: Winter

Best qualities: Energetic, charming, fastidious, sociable, smart, romantic, generous, and honest

Worst qualities: Manipulative, petty, furtive, boring, and power-driven

THE ROMANTIC RAT'S PERSONALITY

In the West, we don't think of rats as being particularly charming. But in the East, the Rat also refers to the hamster, gerbil, guinea pig, and other lovable furry rodents.

Think of a Type-A personality and you'll have a pretty good picture of the industrious Rat. Rats can work from dawn to dusk, digging into one project after another. They are open to new business ventures, socialize easily, and are the life of any party. Rats rarely stop talking, moving, and offering opinions on everything—from cooking to the cosmos.

With their high standards, they are not easily seduced by silly schemes. But they are always ready to talk business if a new opportunity knocks on their door. Rats like to dabble in the stock market, since making money is a top priority.

While generous for the most part, Rats can be greedy when it comes to new acquisitions for themselves. But they are also capable of sudden, elaborate gestures such as buying an expensive gift or offering a luxurious vacation to a close friend or relative. Rats may surprise you when you least expect it with a philanthropy that is typical of their mercurial nature.

Rats are early risers since they are most productive during the morning hours. They are fun-loving characters who like to be involved in the lives of their friends. It's very easy for Rats to become deeply involved in other people's lives, and they are quick to offer a shoulder to cry on when needed. If you have befriended a Rat, you are lucky indeed, for they will stick by you through thick or thin.

While Rats spend a good deal of time ferreting out information about others, they are very secretive about their own personal matters. They may know your entire romantic, financial, and childhood history while you know next to nothing about theirs. Rats often deflect questions about their life like hockey pucks, before gracefully changing the subject.

Family is very important to the Rat. They open their hearts and homes to relatives, even distant ones, letting them stay for long periods of time without paying rent or contributing money to household expenses. However, there's a method behind the Rat's madness. The Rat is calculating a payback. Freeloaders and laggards are put to work, either helping around the house or with the Rat's business ventures.

Beware if you are the employee or coworker of a Rat. Rats like things done correctly the first time. To ensure correct results, Rats stay in control by micromanaging. This may be a problem if you are not used to working under a Rat's close scrutiny; their constant opinions, criticism or nagging may be irritating. Some may see this as a fault. However, when the end result works perfectly, everyone is pleased.

Be careful not to cross a Rat. They don't like being provoked and they are not shy about hiding their feelings when they are. The Rat will give "the look" which says, "back off for now." When hurt, they become tense and impatient. When this happens, they'll snap or hurl an insult. They can also be ambitious and showy in an offensive way. Rats have been known to use their friends to get ahead and later push them aside when they're no longer useful.

The physical, emotional, and mental health of their friends, coworkers, and/or employees are extremely important to the Rat; and it's easy to think they are butting in where they are not wanted. Take it all with a grain of salt. Rats usually have your best interests at heart—their ultimate goal is to have everyone around them become as successful as they are. Rats are always juggling many balls in the air; and since they are so attached to cold, hard cash, it's easy for them to become overextended with work, social obligations, and business affairs.

HER HEART

True to the Rat's nature, a female born under this sign is first and foremost a social creature. She has opinions on every subject and doesn't hold back from expressing them to anyone who will listen. The lady Rat is gregarious—she is constantly extending and receiving party invitations. She's not shy about asking a guy out or being the first to propose a romp in the sack.

Looking good is of utmost importance to the female Rat. She takes pride in her wardrobe and her appearance. When a female Rat walks into the room, all heads turn and stare. They like what they see.

The lady Rat loves to shop, especially when she finds a bargain. She doesn't mind driving out of the way to save a few dollars. The female Rat is happiest when she's buying wholesale, in bulk, or from the sale rack. However, if she sees something she must have or a great gift for someone else, she reaches for her credit card without guilt.

Like the males of this sign, the female Rat is a money magnet—whether she's the CEO, a stay-at-home mom, or the wife of a wealthy man. She brews one viable get-rich-quick scheme after another, and she's savvy at stretching a dollar. Even with a house full of kids, she finds time to work—whether it's a catering service, writing, crafts projects, public relations, or Web designing. She is a clever businesswoman with the mental agility to put a deal together.

Family matters are of utmost importance to the female Rat. She loves her nest and her little ones, as well as her extended family, and she is very close with her siblings. One of her gifts is making the household run smoothly. Dinner is served on time and bedtime is always observed—especially for the kids. The female Rat wants her life, as well as the lives of those around her, to run like clockwork.

When it comes to affairs of the heart, a lady Rat will not put up with bossy, macho men. She has the self-confidence to know she's a great catch. She'll only share her life with Mr. Right. She's a terrific mate with a lot to offer, but she can bend your ear with a litany of sticky little problems. Her mood swings go up and down quicker than a pogo stick. She can say, "Yes, dear," one minute and "No, I want to do it my way," the next. If the female Rat could learn not to sweat the small stuff, life would be a bed of roses for her.

🐀 HIS HEART

Charming and charismatic, the male Rat bears no resemblance to the Western image of a sleazebag or schemer usually associated with this symbolic animal sign.

In Chinese astrology, male Rats are shrewd businessmen, admired for their savvy minds and warm hearts. Perhaps the worst thing to be said is that he works too hard and plays too little; but he is a loyal friend, faithful husband—once he settles down—and fun to be with.

The male Rat's mind is swimming with ideas, especially money-making schemes. Like his female counterpart, he desires material comforts—a large, well-furnished house, a luxury car, state-of-the-art stereo equipment, big-screen television, and the best computer money can buy. This boy likes his toys.

Male Rats are good with math and excel in businesses that call for number-crunching. Their pronounced creative side makes them excellent salesmen, writers, musicians, and artists. Persuasive and tenacious, they can do any job; and once they settle in, they make loyal employees. A male Rat can always be counted on to put in extra time or work on important projects since they are disciplined and well-organized.

He is a born leader who often does best on his own. Of course, not all his business ventures go smoothly; and yet he knows how to pick himself up, dust himself off, and start all over again. His social aptitude means he has a wide network of associates who are eager to help him out when the chips are down.

Although his eyes may roam before he settles down, once he commits, the male Rat can be counted on to be there for you. As a dad, he may get involved in Little League or community matters. But Rats are secretive when they are preoccupied. While they enjoy solving other people's problems, they don't want anyone—including a wife or girlfriend—interfering with theirs. On the plus side, he's a terrific listener and generous with those he loves.

 LUCKY IN LOVE?

Love affairs for the female Rat are necessary for her to reach her ultimate goal—marriage. She's not shy about revealing her feelings, even on a first date. She figures if a guy doesn't want to commit, why bother wasting her time? Some female Rats become desperate after the age of thirty, and they look to unhappily married men as possible mates. The wily female Rat is not beneath stealing someone else's partner. Remember, the nature of the Rat is both social and sly.

Sometimes, even with all her nosing around and dating, the female Rat isn't able to find a companion to settle down with. Then she claims to like being alone. That's not exactly true, but there's no point arguing. She has a retort for every point you bring up. Although she won't admit it, her heart is broken because she wants to be part of a loving family.

The sensual Rat gives herself completely to the right man. Sex is an important part of her life, but it's difficult for her to choose between being a dutiful homemaker and a seductive siren. With gentle coaxing, you can get the female Rat to come out of her protective cocoon and flaunt her wild side. If you want to see her expand her horizons, you have to move slowly. If you push too hard, she may bite.

Although the male Rat will date many women before settling down, he's true to each one while he's with her. He's a flirtatious lover, seducing a woman with compliments. Once you're committed to him, he will expect you to cater to his needs; but he'll make up for it with lavish presents on special occasions.

Don't make the male Rat jealous. He will not tolerate deceit or trickery. Be straightforward with males born under this sign. Honesty and unselfishness are rewarded with tender lovemaking. He is caring, compassionate, and a faithful mate. Even if he withdraws now and then, he will be there for you and the family when you need him.

FOR BETTER OR WORSE

Rat and Ox: This may seem like a lopsided pair, but they are pretty as a picture. The workaholic Rat and the diligent Ox admire each other's qualities. They are both affectionate and willing to demonstrate their romantic feelings. Although the Rat may be more secretive and intense, the Ox doesn't take it personally. If this is you: Your home and family will always be tidy and happy because you work so hard to make it happen.

Rat and Tiger: These two sociable signs complement each other. The Rat wants success and a stable marriage. The Tiger is aggressive but also protective of the family. The Tiger is unpredictable at times and the Rat is secretive, but these are not major issues in an otherwise compatible union. If this is you: You can rely on the fact that you're both committed to the relationship, and your positive outlooks will see you through any obstacles.

Rat and Dragon: This red-hot team is a winner in every way. Together they are a formidable force in business dealings because they work like a well-oiled machine. They always back each other up and present a self-assured, united front. If this is you: You two will enjoy life to the max and get every ounce of pleasure from it.

Rat and Snake: Don't think of the cobra and the mongoose; this mix of opposites does work. The Rat is adventurous and the Snake holds back—both are savvy to the ways of the world. When left alone, they can't keep their hands off each other; and romance plays a large part in their relationship. If this is you: You'll be fine if you can both learn to control your jealousies.

Rat and Monkey: This clever pair are as delicious as champagne and caviar. The Rat is ambitious and so is the Monkey. Together they can overcome any obstacle. Although the Rat is secretive, the Monkey has too many frying pans in the fire to care. When the Monkey is too calculating or frivolous, the Rat deals with it without rancor.

If this is you: Your mutual respect and honesty will mend any problems you have.

Rat and Dog: As long as these two signs keep reinventing the relationship, life is dandy. Both are hardworking, both are homebodies. Affection is not a problem, but boredom is. While this pair is compatible, the union may seem stale after a few years unless each continues to develop new interests. If this is you: You two will need to ignore your homebody inclinations and travel the world to keep boredom away.

Rat and Rat: Too much of a good thing makes a disagreeable mix. Two Type-A personalities trying to work together and raise a family is very intense. They both want to be on top, which means nobody is minding the store. Of course, two Rats are savvy in business and passionate about each other. If this is you: You two will need to put in a lot of effort to keep the power balanced.

Rat and Rabbit: The Rat is too intense, and the Rabbit is too passive, so there's no push-and-pull. The Rabbit finds the Rat overbearing and distant. The Rat finds the Rabbit too disinterested and needy. The strain will take its toll even though there is genuine love between them. If this is you: You two will need to get over your self-centered tendencies in order to give this relationship a chance.

Rat and Horse: The Rat's intense spirit will get on the Horse's nerves and small arguments will escalate into major battles. The Rat tends to find fault and the Horse doesn't like it. A house full of children will provide another source of friction. If this is you: You two should seek outside help to learn how to manage your differences without arguing so much.

Rat and Sheep: The overzealous, materialistic Rat is no match for the sensitive, artistic Sheep. This relationship may work for a while, especially if the Rat indulges the Sheep's every whim. But that routine gets old in a hurry and the irritations will start, like a piece of sand in an oyster. If this is you: You'll be okay if the Rat makes an effort to tone down his/her zealousness and the Sheep tries to be more focused.

Rat and Rooster: Nothing the Rat can do pleases the fussy Rooster. Instead of being affectionate and understanding, the Rooster wants to figure things out, which causes trouble whenever these two are together. Family is not a top priority for the Rooster, which causes even more friction. If this is you: You two will need to make a big compromise—the Rooster needs to hold his/her critical tongue and the Rat needs to let go of some of his/her need for control—or you'll build too much resentment to make it work.

Rat and Pig: This is one of those borderline relationships where it will take diligence to keep it together. Both are fun-loving individuals who like nice things. However, one may go overboard in the quest for fun and excitement, which makes the other party unhappy. If this is you: You two need to keep each other on the same page by focusing on having fun together—find a class, a hobby, or a sport you both enjoy and devote yourselves to keeping your passion alive.

 ## WRITTEN IN THE STARS

Celebrity unions are fairly easy to analyze when we see them in terms of the Chinese zodiac. Since most people are familiar with the players, let's see what went wrong with this couple.

Gwyneth Paltrow, born September 28, 1972, is a Rat. She's the daughter of actress Blythe Danner and producer Bruce Paltrow. She made her first film, *Shout*, in 1991; and because of her innate social and energetic personality, she was destined to become a major-league actress. She met Brad Pitt on the set of *Seven* in 1995, and a year later they were engaged. But, ultimately, they broke off the engagement.

Born on December 18, 1963, Brad Pitt is a Rabbit—the Rat and the Rabbit aren't the best match. The major problem in this pairing is that the Rat is too intense and the Rabbit is too passive. The Rabbit finds the Rat overbearing and distant. The Rat finds the Rabbit too disinterested and needy. The strain will take its toll even if there is genuine love between them. Gwyneth admitted she was devastated when she said: "When we split up, my heart sort of broke that day, and it will never be the same."

On the rebound, she began dating Ben Affleck,

whom she met on the set of *Shakespeare in Love*. The two were inseparable for nearly two years. But Affleck, born August 15, 1972, is also a Rat—and two Rats are a disagreeable mix.

Rats are classic Type-A individuals—competition between them is very intense. With their mega-star careers in overdrive, friction between Gwyneth and Ben was inevitable.

Gwyneth Paltrow was a stunning match with both Brad and Ben; but the power of her destiny, combined with the stresses of stardom, took its toll on their relationships. Sometimes it's easier to let go and move on, which is apparently what these stars decided to do. Hopefully, this pretty, talented actress will find happiness with a compatible sign from the Chinese zodiac.

The Steady Ox

Years of the Ox: 1901, 1913, 1925, 1937, 1949, 1961, 1973, 1985, and 1997

Famous Oxen: Johann Sebastian Bach, Robert Redford, Dustin Hoffman, Bill Cosby, Jim Carrey, Carson Daly, and Mary Tyler Moore

Season: Winter

Best qualities: Patient, industrious, noble, precise, reserved, self-sacrificing, tenacious, and strong

Worst qualities: Sluggish, rigid, obstinate, jealous, unforgiving, and despotic

THE STEADY OX'S PERSONALITY

The Ox is methodical, sensible, and a bit dull at times. The Ox is a follower, not a leader, and prefers to be a member of the pack. The Ox's best quality is reliability—he can be counted on through thick and thin.

Taking a closer look at this trustworthy, tried and true friend, we see that the Ox is patient and a good listener. The problem is that the Ox can be stubborn and undemonstrative to a fault.

The personality traits of the Ox are closely linked with the animal itself in this case. While the Ox prefers to be passive, when a situation arises that needs attention, the Ox jumps right in to address the problem. A calm and rational person, the Ox takes charge of the moment, then hands over the reins of leadership to someone else and retreats to the middle of the pack, where they feel most comfortable.

The Ox is a linear thinker. If there is a problem, it will be solved. Period. End of case. The Ox is not a deep thinker, nor is he or she untruthful or deceptive. The Ox is as honest as the day is long. "Don't ask for an opinion if you really don't want to hear the truth," says the affable Ox. Methodical, cautious, and slow to react, the Ox plods along, taking in all the details and chewing them like cud. No point is unobserved, undetected, or unexplored. The Ox weighs all factors before making a decision—including in matters of love. If you're in a hurry, forget it. Meticulous to the point of distraction, the Ox wants all ducks in a row before making a commitment—whether in business or in romance. The Ox is slow to commit—if he or she commits at all. They truly don't leave anything to chance. Once the Ox has decided to trust a situation, however, he or she is a loyal partner who will protect his own, care for the family, and bolster his or her friends both emotionally and financially.

Be careful never to cross an Ox. Although Oxen usually have tremendous control over their emotions, if you push them too far, things can get ugly. Oxen are capable of being fearsome and frightening—they may throw things or put a fist through a wall if they are provoked. And they will hold grudges for slights and past hurts—they may not be emotional, but still waters run deep.

Despite their stern exterior, Oxen have a sense of humor that, once turned on, is a joy to behold. It's easy to forgive Oxen, even though they can be stubborn pains at times, because they are always so capable, dependable, and honest. What's not to like?

 **HER HEART**

The female Ox is a devoted mom who can whip up an apple pie or a five-course meal at the drop of a hat. She runs a tight ship at home—her children are so well behaved she can take them into a shop containing the most delicate china without incident. In addition to all of her hard, meticulous work, the lady Ox always has time to spare for her honey—in fact, it's her top priority.

The female Ox is a tough cookie who isn't in need of any outside help. If her man leaves, she won't sit around whining. Instead, she will make it her business to raise the kids, join the PTA, and carry out her social obligations, and hold down a job, without a hitch. There's no stopping the steady female Ox—she doesn't need a man to make her feel complete.

Says the lady Ox: "I am woman and don't forget it."

Despite her independence, the female Ox is a softy at heart. If her man strays, she will wait until his passion is spent and then welcome him back. While she may hold a grudge for a long while, her inner strength will buoy her through the most turbulent seas.

Beware of getting too comfortable! The lady Ox cannot tolerate laziness or sloppiness. She's judgmental of herself and others. Despite this stubborn side of her personality, you'll find it difficult to be annoyed for very long—her friendly, outgoing demeanor and genuine caring for others will turn you around every time. This is a take-charge lady who shoulders responsibility without complaint.

 ## HIS HEART

The male Ox likes doing home repairs; but because he's so slow, it may take forever until he gets around to fixing a problem. Tinkering with the car and puttering around the garage are his favorite weekend pastimes. He takes pride in mending broken things, but he'd rather not tackle a long, involved project.

Even though the male Ox isn't one to openly profess his love, he will do something nice for you—wash your car, buy a new appliance for the house, or clean the garage. Romance isn't his strong point, but at least you can take comfort in the fact that he will make a terrific dad and a steady partner. For the male Ox, family is of the utmost importance—not only his immediate family, but all of his relatives as well.

The male Ox is cautious with business dealings and money—including going overboard on frivolous purchases—like a luxury car, expensive house, or costly vacation—yet when it comes to food, he'll spare no expense.

While the men born under this sign think it's okay to stray now and then—since "it doesn't mean anything"—if you cheat on one of them, don't get caught. He doesn't take infidelity lightly—unless it's his own. He will vent his anger and hold it against you for ages.

The male Ox is a stern taskmaster with his children. Although he loves them deeply and would do anything for them, his rules and expectations often seem callous and unfair.

Keep in mind that getting the male Ox to do something may seem like pushing against a brick wall. Not only is he stubborn, but he's also not shy about voicing his opinion. So you'll need patience to cope with his occasionally obstinate behavior. Remember that under his stodgy exterior, he is a sweet guy and that a little praise goes a long way in winning his heart.

 **LUCKY IN LOVE?**

Passion isn't uppermost in the minds of either Mr. or Ms. Ox. They simply want to be out of the dating game and in a solid relationship where they can let their hair down and stop pretending to be something they are not. You won't find the female Ox primping and preening to make an impression on a guy—her true beauty is in her self-assurance. She relies on her spunky spirit to win a man's heart. She's not a flirt or a minx—she's a sturdy, no-nonsense woman—and a guy will know right from the start whether she's interested or not.

Don't think that this lady can be bedded easily. She may even withhold sex until she has a firm commitment or a ring on her finger. While she won't be dressed up in a sexy lace nighty or a garter belt and stockings, her earthy passion is a delight for any lover.

Unlike the female Ox, who is usually content to be a homebody once she is married, the male Ox doesn't feel that he should be limited to one partner. He will support his family and be there for them through thick and thin. But if an opportunity for sex comes along, he will be sorely tempted and may follow through—if the conditions are right. His object isn't to hurt anyone, it's strictly self-gratification and a boost to his ego. Once in awhile, a female Ox can have this same trait. Woe to the person who has a fling with the Ox. She will quickly find out that love and sex do not go hand in hand for this man. Sex is sex—he loves his wife. A woman could hold her breath for twenty years waiting for him to dump his family for her—it will probably never happen.

 ## FOR BETTER OR WORSE

Ox and Rat: This may seem like a lopsided pair, but they are pretty as a picture. The workaholic Rat and the diligent

Ox admire each other's qualities. They are both affectionate and willing to demonstrate their romantic feelings. Although the Rat may be more secretive and intense, the Ox doesn't take it personally. If this is you: Your home and family will always be tidy and happy.

Ox and Ox: Laboring through life, two Oxen make an agreeable pair without overwhelming passion. As the family grows, romance becomes less important to the female Ox and the male may stray. Since both bottle up their emotions, lack of communication could take its toll unless they resolve unsettled issues. If this is you: You two need to make pleasure a big priority so you aren't consumed by work, but don't forget to exercise!

Ox and Dragon: This couple will struggle for power. While it might not seem that this is a good mix at first glance, these two signs are surprisingly alike. The Ox can be stubborn and slow while the Dragon can be pushy and fast-moving, making an ongoing give-and-take a necessity. As long as they give each other enough space and nip problems in the bud, their relationship can last. If this is you: You'll be sure to thrive so long as you nip problems in the bud by keeping the lines of communication open.

Ox and Snake: The Snake likes the fortitude of the dependable Ox. The Ox is patient and rational and prevents the Snake from taking absurd risks. The Snake appreciates the Ox's logic and steadfastness and is willing to work long and hard to please the Ox—the Ox returns the favor. If this is you: You can learn a lot from your partner, so practice tolerance and try not to be annoyed by petty problems.

Ox and Rooster: The dependable Ox and the pushy Rooster work together well if they have a common goal. The Rooster may pick on the Ox, but the Ox doesn't care. The Rooster is a determined go-getter, and the Ox has lofty goals and works steadily toward them. If this is you: You two need to remember to stoke the fires of love and keep the passion alive or things might fizzle down to friendship.

Ox and Dog: This is a borderline case—the two signs can get along, but it requires flexibility on both parts. The Dog is idealistic, while the Ox digs in his heels. The Dog may find the Ox too unyielding, and the Ox may find the Dog too sociable. However, if they use their combined energies for a common goal, like raising a family or working for a just cause, they can accomplish any task. If this is you: You two have to readjust your pace and find a common stride— you just need a little give and take, and things will work out.

Ox and Tiger: Take two individuals with a heady temper, put them together, and watch the fireworks explode. The Tiger lets loose with volatile emotions while the Ox takes it all in, bottling up emotions until they are at the boiling point. The Ox's slow demeanor will drive the frisky Tiger crazy. If this is you: You two need to learn how to compromise! Don't be afraid to seek outside help—it's sure to help you both understand your quirky union.

Ox and Rabbit: There's only one question to ask of this couple: Where's the passion? The Rabbit is shy and reserved, the Ox is emotionally controlled. The Rabbit values friendships as well as family, but the Ox is not really a people person. If this is you: You may be in for a bumpy ride. Your uneven match will need a lot of effort and compromise if you're going to make it work.

Ox and Horse: No love is lost between this pair. The methodical Ox follows the rules and sticks with the herd while the spirited Horse sprints ahead. The Ox will take the long road and the Horse will look for any shortcut. Harsh words cause wounds, grudges are held, and communication breaks down. If this is you: You two only have two choices if you want this to work: either learn to hold your tongue or blabber it all to a professional who'll help you sort it out by focusing on the good—not the bad.

Ox and Sheep: The sensitive Sheep is 180 degrees from the Ox, which puts them at odds. The Sheep enjoys spending freely and prefers to live lavishly. The Ox, on the other hand, is frugal and wants to live simply. If this is you: You'll need to find a middle ground by negotiating your financial goals from the outset. If you don't, you'll be so blinded by money that you'll miss out on each other.

Ox and Monkey: Mixing a clever, outgoing Monkey with a stubborn, slow-moving Ox creates a lot of trouble. The Monkey is too quick-witted for the methodical Ox. The only way to make this union work is if each accepts the other without trying to change the innate personality. If this is you: You'll probably need outside help in order to find some common ground.

Ox and Pig: The personalities of these two signs can be compatible, but they're not great in the romance department. The Ox is domineering while the Pig likes to have a good time with friends. Although the Pig may seem too frivolous for the serious Ox, they both share a robust love for the good life. If this is you: You two can work this out with love and a lot of patience.

 WRITTEN IN THE STARS

Celebrity unions are fairly easy to analyze when we see them in terms of the Chinese zodiac. Since most people are familiar with the players, let's see what happened to this celebrity couple.

Actress Meg Ryan was born November 19, 1961, making her an Ox. The blue-eyed cutie attended Bethel High School in New York, where she was prom queen, and majored in journalism at college. To earn extra money, she took up acting. It was a terrific career move! Her debut was playing Candice Bergen's daughter in the movie *Rich and Famous* in 1981. She moved to Hollywood in 1984. In 1987, Meg met her future husband, Dennis Quaid, on the set of *Innerspace*. Ryan and Quaid married in 1991 and had one child—Jack Henry.

Dennis Quaid was born April 9, 1954, in Houston

and studied drama in college, but dropped out before finishing his studies. As a Horse, he is a free spirit. This wasn't a match made in heaven. The steady Ox, Meg Ryan, plays by the rules while Quaid marches to his own beat. This can drive a female Ox to distraction—and after nine years of marriage, that's what happened.

While making the movie *Proof of Life* in 1999, Meg Ryan left her marriage for the film's male lead actor, Russell Crowe—born April 7, 1964—a Dragon. The Ox and the Dragon are very well suited to each other, but the relationship had too much baggage and fizzled shortly after it began.

Unfortunately, Ryan and Quaid were not able to reconcile. The Horse can be a hothead and unforgiving and the Ox is stubborn and vindictive—nothing could put the marriage of Hollywood's golden couple back together again.

The Sexy Tiger

Years of the Tiger: 1902, 1914, 1926, 1938, 1950, 1962, 1974, 1986, and 1998

Famous Tigers: Ludwig von Beethoven, Queen Elizabeth II, Marilyn Monroe, Garth Brooks, Tom Cruise, and Stevie Wonder

Season: Winter

Best qualities: Generous, brave, honest, fascinating, strong, receptive, smart, and earnest

Worst qualities: Vain, brash, disrespectful, combative, foolhardy, and careless

THE SEXY TIGER'S PERSONALITY

The Tiger personality is an amazing blend of many marvelous traits. Tigers are great people to be around—they are filled with a zest for life and spread cheer to everyone in their company. Their terrific senses of humor enable them to laugh at anything—including themselves. Their hearts are always in the right place—with family and friends first in the order of priorities. Tigers thrive on being surrounded by loved ones—they extend this invitation to people and animals alike, thus you'll probably find many pets in their homes.

Boredom is not a word in the average Tiger's vocabulary—that's part of their incredible charm. There's something going on every minute of their day. They love change, and it's not unusual for them to make spontaneous purchases, trade in their car on a whim, or go house shopping even though their present abode is perfectly adequate. They relish change to such a large extent, that even before they move in, their plans for renovations are already in the works. They will tirelessly work side by side with the construction crew to make sure everything is taken care of—down to the last nail—and as soon as the project is complete, they're on to something new.

Tigers are prone to the blues. During these "down" times—which don't last long—Tigers need some TLC. They don't expect you to solve their problems, they simply need someone to listen and provide sympathy or compassion—whatever is needed to bring back their sunny disposition. There is no point giving Tigers advice—they follow their own heart. They're wise enough to know that there is a solution for every problem, and they are determined to overcome every obstacle on their own.

Intense, headstrong, and often inflexible, the Tiger is very particular about how projects are completed. Their favorite expression is: "Let's do it my way." They don't like to be told what to do or when to do it. Beware of crossing them—they have fierce snarls. When bruised, the Tiger's claws come out, along with a tirade of noxious and hurtful barbs. Their view of all things—especially business, litigation, and projects that involve brute strength—is all or nothing; so, if you don't want to get hurt, you should stand back and let them go to work.

Tigers of both sexes are independent and dependable. They are territorial—staking out their claim and defending it ferociously against intruders. And they are impulsive—taking risks with crazy schemes or ill-timed financial investments. Tigers live on the edge, which makes close friends and relatives crazy. It takes a strong heart to be with Tigers, especially when they appear flighty with their lives or finances. But be assured, Tigers will not put others in jeopardy; in fact, just the opposite is true. Tigers are protectors and defenders who will make you feel safe in their presence.

Independent by nature, Tigers like to be petted but not confined by marriage or monogamous relationships. Any male who is hooked up with a Tigress should give her plenty of room to "do her thing." Likewise, any female who wants to be with a male Tiger should be aware of his shortcomings with commitments. If you're together for the endorphin rush that romance brings, that's all well and fine; but a word of warning: Don't be disappointed if things don't work out for the long run.

If you're fortunate enough to have a Tiger as a mate, you'll find a committed partner who will give 100 percent to the relationship. If you want to set up shop with a Tiger, you'll have to make sure that the wild flings are over. Tigers express themselves with reckless abandon in their early years, traveling, skydiving, snowboarding, or putting themselves in peril. It's enough to make your heart stop. As they mature, they settle down to some degree. Should the opportunity for adventure present itself, don't be surprised if your Tiger mate is off and running for one more wild escapade.

At home Tigers need space. They are high-energy people who are happiest when doing two or three things at a time—Tigers are masters at multitasking.

HER HEART

Because of her independent nature, the female Tiger often prefers the single life. If she gets married and has children, it may not last very long—and she'll probably spend long stretches of time between mates. The Tiger can entertain herself in style. Just give her a hammer or a camera, and she will stay busy for days on end. If a man offers to help, she'll shrug off his overture with a cool, "Thanks, but no thanks."

As a mom, she's tops. She is devoted, protective, and caring. She also gives her cubs plenty of space to grow.

Unlike the lady Ox, who spends her spare time in the kitchen and laundry room, the female Tiger would rather leave the housework and take her kids on a nature trip instead.

The Tigress, her children, and her mate operate in a world of mutual understanding, peace, and space. As long as everyone is respectful of this delicate balance, life is simply grand. If crossed, the Tigress will pounce; and she is not one to forgive easily.

The Tigress wants to challenge life and herself. She pushes hard in the male-dominated world of business. She is always ready to take on any project—and toil longer and harder than her male coworkers.

On the other hand, she is a seductress. There is nothing masculine about ladies born under this sign. Dressing for success is one way to get what she really wants. This is a woman with purpose, no deceit, and with dreams of rising, like cream, to the top. The Tigress must beware, however, not to lose control when she is stressed. Her lack of patience can rock the boat, especially in business dealings.

Her social graces are superb. With charm and wit, she doesn't mince words. After blurting out a sarcastic remark, she'll laugh and say: "Don't you get it—that was a joke!" Even while she's playing around, she's critiquing everyone with a practiced eye—taking mental notes—which she'll use in the future to propel her forward on her quest for accomplishment.

The Tigress makes a loyal friend and an exciting lover. Married men are not off limits, and she may have two lovers at the same time, with no intention of marrying either of them! She doesn't like rejection nor does she like to be possessed—her independent nature makes her want to do things her way. She may seem unpredictable and impulsive, but there is usually a method to her madness. Win or lose at love, the Tigress is a survivor who knows that another suitor is always around the corner.

🐅 HIS HEART

Don't even think about trying to compromise with a male Tiger. When the going gets tough, he switches into high gear and drives himself, and everyone around him, nuts in the process. The male Tiger succeeds with his endeavors nearly all of the time. When he fails, he goes into the lair to lick his wounds and figure out another way to tackle the project. The bigger the challenge, the better he likes it. He thrives on the thrill of victory—and cannot cope with the agony of defeat. The male Tiger is the classic over-achiever. With his glib tongue and confident air, he makes an excellent salesman or CEO.

The male Tiger surrounds himself with boy toys: computer gadgetry, stereo systems, and fast cars. He's not thrifty when it comes to his own desires and thinks nothing of blowing his budget. He knows he will rise to the challenge if he overspends.

The Tiger is a charming guy but he's prideful, over-confident, and a workaholic. He's not concerned about what others think. He goes his merry way making things work on his agenda and for his ultimate purpose. He chooses his friends very carefully—he adamantly requires loyalty, integrity, respect, and honesty from those close to him.

The male Tiger is a romantic at heart. He's a passionate lover who knows how to woo a female. Once he commits his heart, he enjoys showing his lady off to everyone—that's why he prowls for gorgeous babes. He may even offer to pay for a cosmetic procedure for the lady of his dreams. Some gals will eagerly accept, others will find this a turn-off, but try not to hold it against him— it's just his nature.

Is he a tiger in the sack? Yes, if you don't try to tame him. This man needs to roam, which can wreck the best relationship. Like the Tigress, he wants his space and the freedom to come and go as he pleases. If you're smart, you'll enjoy the company of this suave, handsome guy without crowding him. He will not tolerate being dominated. His romantic attachments tend to be short-lived— even when a relationship ends, he has the unique ability to remain on good terms with his past lovers. Despite his aversion to feeling trapped, he makes a terrific, encouraging, and committed father, encouraging his kids to take part in sports and applauding their academic achievements.

LUCKY IN LOVE?

The female Tiger is sleek and alluring—constantly preening and fussing over her appearance. She moves steadily from one lover to another, greedy for more, and heady with the experience. While she doesn't exhibit jealousy, she is keenly aware of a man's emotional attachment. If it's too strong, she will break it off. The Tigress doesn't take rejection well; so if you're thinking of dumping her, get ready to run. She demands a very fine balance of mutual respect and admiration.

The male Tiger loves the thrill of the chase. Making love to many women shows his prowess, and he's ready to brag at length about his conquests. If you take up with him, know that you'll be talked about in the locker room and at the water cooler. Don't expect to take this macho guy shopping at the mall or try to tame him. He's not going to hold your purse while you try on clothes! However, if you want wild adventures—this is the man for you.

FOR BETTER OR WORSE

Tiger and Rat: These two sociable signs complement each other. The Tiger is unpredictable at times and the Rat is secretive, but these are not major issues. The Rat wants success and a stable family life. The Tiger is aggressive but also protective of the family. They are both committed to raising children. If this is you: Your positive outlook will help you succeed.

Tiger and Horse: The goal-oriented Tiger and the free-spirited but ambitious Horse get along well together. They are both strong, bold, impulsive, and open to new ideas. They are also both smart enough to give the other plenty of space. Both are honest, and the connection is excellent between these two extroverts. If this is you: Make sure you are both headed in the same direction to make this union last.

Tiger and Sheep: This is not a hot-blooded union. However, they can be fast friends since the Sheep is sympathetic when the Tiger needs comforting, and the Tiger is protective and concerned about the Sheep's welfare. If this is you: You two may not be destined for love, but you're so compatible that a long-term friendship is definitely in your future.

Tiger and Rooster: Neither of these signs shies away from controversy, which works to their mutual advantage. The Tiger, who may be more diplomatic and charming than the hot-tempered Rooster, admires the Rooster's enthusiasm and lust for living. The Rooster enjoys being out in social situations with the suave, smooth-talking Tiger. If this is you: You'll both be living it up and loving life as long as you can learn to talk out petty problems.

Tiger and Dog: The affectionate Dog is awed by the Tiger's strength and power. The Dog plays by the rules, which the Tiger respects; and when the Tiger's ego begins blowing out of proportion, the Dog brings it down to Earth by nipping the Tiger's temper in the bud. If this is you: You may go up and down like a roller coaster, but the bond between you is as strong as cement.

Tiger and Pig: In the wild, the Tiger would gobble the Pig for breakfast and never think twice. Yet in the Chinese zodiac, this is one of the best matches. They are both social and honest. The Pig is forgiving, and the Tiger likes to be forgiven for silly indiscretions. The Pig thinks the Tiger is awesome, and the Tiger feels relaxed and comfortable in the presence of the Pig. They are passionate and spontaneous in the bedroom and in the boardroom. If this is you: You two can chalk this relationship up as a winner—not that you're likely to do much resting!

Tiger and Ox: The Ox's slow, plodding demeanor will drive the Tiger to distraction. These two want different things from life, and neither will budge an inch. The Tiger lets loose with a barrage of insults while the Ox takes it all in, fuming inside until all hell breaks loose. If this is you: You'll both need to invest a lot of effort on managing your volatile temperaments—if you learn to focus on the good, it may just work out.

Tiger and Tiger: Although these two felines are compatible to some extent, they are too much alike to ever really get along. Both want their independence and neither wants to change. Petty annoyances eat away at their relationship. If children are involved, they will often be the pivotal point in an ugly tug-of-war. If this is you: You two need to remember that life is too short for such squabbling.

Tiger and Rabbit: The Tiger is too temperamental for the peace-loving placid Rabbit. The Rabbit will run and hide when the Tiger unleashes a tirade—making for very poor communication between them. And the Rabbit's emotional ups and downs grate on the Tiger's nerves. If this is you: You'll both need to compromise. If the Tiger can tone it down and the Rabbit can gain a modicum of self-confidence, you may have a shot at making this a fruitful union.

Tiger and Dragon: These two feisty signs are both powerful individuals, secure in themselves, which spells trouble unless they learn that life is a give and take. Moderation is the key to a successful union with this pair. While they present a smooth facade to the outside world, a struggle for domination is going on within the union. If this is you: You two will never get along unless you emphasize mutual respect and cooperation.

Tiger and Snake: The Snake is threatened by the Tiger's strength and outgoing attitude. The Snake prefers to curl up with a good book or video, while the Tiger wants to prowl. To the Tiger, the Snake seems cool, detached, and positively unenthusiastic. The result is a battleground of conflict and misunderstanding. If this is you: You two will need to cool it down and learn how to accentuate the positive if you want to stay together.

Tiger and Monkey: The Monkey is 180 degrees in opposition to the Tiger, which puts them at odds. Tigers use power and strength to get what they want. The clever Monkey uses cunning and trickery. Both are ambitious and both are sore losers. It seems inevitable that these two will set themselves up in competition, and the relationship may buckle under the strain unless intervention is sought. If this is you: You need to find separate activities or seek outside help—if you try to compete with each other, you'll lose the relationship.

WRITTEN IN THE STARS

Celebrity unions are fairly easy to analyze when we see them in terms of the Chinese zodiac. Since most people are familiar with the players, let's see why this popular couple gets along.

In 1984, television newscaster Connie Chung, born August 20, 1946, under the sign of the Dog, married talk-show host Maury Povich, born January 17, 1939, under the sign of the Tiger. Nearly twenty years later, they are still very much married. So let's see what made this relationship work.

According to the Chinese zodiac, the loyal Dog is awed by the Tiger's strength and power. Povich is a major player in the field of daytime television. Connie gave up her anchor position with the nightly news to raise a family. The Dog plays by the rules, which the Tiger respects. When the Tiger's ego begins blowing out of proportion, the Dog brings it down to Earth. These statements seem to be true of this entertainment couple. When Povich's show gets too sleazy, Connie tells him to tone it down. Whatever goes on behind closed doors with this dynamic pair, it's obvious to all that the bond between them is still very strong.

The Perceptive Rabbit

Years of the Rabbit: 1903, 1915, 1927, 1939, 1951, 1963, 1975, 1987, and 1999

Famous Rabbits: Napoleon Bonaparte, Albert Einstein, Bob Hope, Jane Seymour, Tina Turner, Lisa Kudrow, and Drew Barrymore

Season: Spring

Best qualities: Practical, cautious, sensitive, tactful, friendly, hospitable, bright, and talented

Worst qualities: Old-fashioned, reserved, aloof, worrisome, touchy, defensive, and secretive

THE PERCEPTIVE
RABBIT'S PERSONALITY

Sometimes called the Cat, the Rabbit is considered to be born under a lucky sign. They are excellent judges of character and difficult to deceive, hence the term "perceptive." Although introverted when alone, Rabbits come to life in the company of others—interaction with groups bolsters their self-esteem.

Rabbits usually have a sunny disposition. They are soft-spoken, gentle, and compassionate. Anyone with a Rabbit as a friend, life partner, or lover should consider themselves blessed. Rabbits enjoy quiet, uncluttered lives and appreciate the beauty of nature, as well as having a close circle of friends.

Rabbits do not like direct confrontations or challenges. And yet under their quiet exteriors are self-possessed, strong-willed individuals who pursue one goal after another with careful precision. Don't let their self-effacing manners fool you—Rabbits aren't pushovers. Just because Rabbits don't swear up a storm, rant and rage, throw temper tantrums, or conduct hostile takeovers doesn't mean they're content to sit around chewing on carrot sticks.

In business, Rabbits are powerful and shrewd negotiators. Using the suave wine-and-dine-them approach, Rabbits get exactly what they are after without a huge fuss. There is no whistle-blowing or fireworks. Once the deal is done, Rabbits proceed quietly on their merry ways—contracts signed, sealed, and delivered.

Although Rabbits may appear slow to make decisions

and a bit awkward in social situations, they are actually just deliberate and cautious by nature—they aren't dopes. These intelligent individuals read the fine print before signing on the dotted line. Very little escapes the resourceful Rabbit.

Rabbits may be moody at times, but this is simply their nature. They tend to shoulder heavy burdens without complaint or bitterness. It's natural for depression to creep in now and then, but it rarely lasts long. A spontaneous get-together, a night out, a party, a movie, or a sporting event will make Rabbits lively once again.

Rabbits' most impressive trait is their limitless capacity for sympathy. They are superb caregivers, compassionate therapists, and excellent moderators and mediators. They are wonderful friends, always willing to lend an ear—or money. Everyone respects the Rabbit's sage advice, and the Rabbit enjoys giving it.

Bunnies like to live well without breaking the bank. Well-tailored clothing, a spacious home, and a dependable car are on their agenda. Above all, harmony must prevail at home, at work, in social contacts, and in business matters. Rabbits will quickly back off if dissention is rampant or a confrontation is imminent.

Both male and female Rabbits need space in relationships—don't crowd them in with too many obligations and commitments. A little leeway goes a long way.

🐰 HER HEART

She's not a gold-digger, but the lady Rabbit doesn't mind the idea of marrying someone with plenty of dough. After

all, she likes nice things—especially silk, cashmere, manicures, pedicures, or relaxing at the spa. While living well is
important, Rabbits can also be happy with less, as long as
peace prevails.

Lady Rabbits always have empathy and hugs for
underdogs. Although they can be counted on to stand up
for their friends and family, don't expect them to lead any
crusades. While they are feminists at heart, they're not mil-
itant and they don't like large crowds or confrontations.
On the other hand, female Rabbits aren't doormats either—
and won't be pushed around.

Unflappable and rational, she is a near-perfect balance. If the Rabbit gets overwrought at times and throws
a tantrum or falls into a funk, it will pass like a rainstorm
on a summer day, and her sunny disposition will soon
return.

Although female Rabbits are successful in their profes-
sions, they usually prefer to be homemakers—but they
don't mind working part-time or from their home, which is
always decorated with charm.

The Rabbit appears shy, which is a turn-on for many
men. Although she can be self-sufficient, she wants
someone to take care of her and to cuddle with her at
night. She needs to feel safe from harm—she is fearful of
burglars and muggers. Taking a self-defense course or carrying pepper spray is a good idea for a lady Rabbit. It will
make her feel less anxious.

Female Rabbits will not tolerate abusive mates,
screamers, or anyone who threatens their physical or emotional well-being. They don't want to be criticized or

degraded in any way. They demand respect for themselves and their children.

Even if your lady Rabbit is not a robust or exciting lover—and rarely initiates sex—you can be sure that she is a faithful mate and a devoted wife. The female Rabbit is a lucky catch.

🐇 HIS HEART

The male Rabbit is a great guy. He's polite, charming, witty; and you'll usually find him surrounded by plenty of friends. If you think you can have him all to yourself, think again. He's a man's man who loves women. These charismatic characters light up a room with their presence. He is easygoing, except when crossed, and enjoys the good life: fine wines, nice cars, trendy duds, and expensive meals in high-class restaurants. And there's nothing wrong with that, if he can afford it.

Male Rabbits tend to be lucky in business and in love. Their genial nature attracts investors to their trade or profession, and they are astute negotiators. Rabbits take orders well and like an organized routine, which makes them good accountants, teachers, scholars, or scientists. With an uncanny sixth sense, perceptive male Rabbits speculate on the stock market, business ventures, or games in a casino with astonishing accuracy. The good news is that they know when to stop and walk away with a profit—instead of blowing their cash in a frenzy of poor choices.

Professionally and romantically, the male Rabbit takes

the high road and doesn't demean himself in petty squabbles or shouting matches. Few things are so important that he will lose his cool. Like his female counterparts, the male Rabbits value harmony and peace within his environment.

As a friend, the male Rabbit is the best—unless you take advantage of him, in which case you'll find a cold shoulder instead of a sympathetic one. He's an easy mark for down-on-their-luck pals and kinfolk. He'll oblige to a point, then it's "Sorry, man, I can't"—by that he means he won't.

Financially, the male Rabbit has the potential to make oodles of money and he will, given time. He's not a pushy fellow and he knows that everything happens in due time. That goes for love also. When the time is right, he will make a commitment. He is a great dad and enjoys spending time with his offspring at basketball, hockey, or football games.

🐰 LUCKY IN LOVE?

The female Rabbit looks for someone who will provide stability and support in a harmonious union. Raising children is part of her long-term plan; and even on a first date, she will size up a man's potential to provide her with the home environment she needs. She wants a man who is worthy of her esteem; and she, in turn, desires to be with a partner who will respect her. Once she settles down, the household will run like clockwork. Her culinary skills are topnotch, and she has everything under control—even if she's also holding down a part-time or full-time job.

Plenty of women throw themselves at the male Rabbit's foot, but he's holding out for that one special gal—the one who will accept his heart and soul. He may appear arrogant and vain because of his standoffishness and reluctance to make a commitment. He is cautious about being tied down, and he will break numerous hearts before settling in with Ms. Right. The Rabbit man is jittery to a fault—he wants to make the correct choice before saying "I do." He needs someone who will work into his life plan, not a showpiece. Male Rabbits rarely complain that they can't find a woman to love. If anything, their caring nature makes them babe magnets—they have too many choices. Will he be faithful? If the relationship is harmonious, there's no reason for him to stray. But if the shouting matches begin, the male Rabbit would rather be alone than with a shrew.

 ## FOR BETTER OR WORSE

Rabbit and Rabbit: These like personalities get along famously. Both the male and female of this sign are mindful of each other's feelings. Neither wants to argue, fuss, or fight. Both want a home filled with love and children, and both have an innate sixth sense so they know intuitively if something is amiss with the other. If this is you: You two are at the top of everyone's invitation list—who wouldn't want such a fun-loving, easygoing couple around?

Rabbit and Dragon: This unlikely duo has the potential to make it work. The Dragon may be overbearing at times, but as long as there is no yelling or violence, the Rabbit can deal with it. Problems need to be addressed when they occur and not left to fester, which is something the Rabbit likes to do. As long as the quiet Rabbit understands that the Dragon is naturally blustery and doesn't take it personally, this union may last for the long run. If this is you: When problems arise, try to understand your partner's point of view without being judgmental.

Rabbit and Snake: This pair will have plenty of ups and downs. The Snake is not always forthcoming with compliments or with help around the house. It may feel as though the Rabbit is carrying the burden of the relationship. However, with open communication and a nonjudgmental attitude, this union can work out just fine.

Rabbit and Sheep: These two have the same attachments to comfort and appreciation of nature's beauty. Their souls beat as one with compassion and sympathy. Together the Rabbit and Sheep want to make the world a better place in which to live. They will adopt children or open their hearts to foster kids to make one big, happy family. If this is you: You two have the magic touch—you're truly soul mates.

Rabbit and Dog: These two likable signs make a good team. Both are loyal and devotedly attached to one another. They are social and committed to making this a better world. The basic stability of each individual means this union has the potential to last many years—both partners are in it for the long run. If this is you: You'll be the envy of all your friends for your love has the ability to endure.

Rabbit and Pig: Talk about complementing each other. The Pig is generous in spirit and with money. The Rabbit is considerate and affectionate. Both like a good party and an active social life. Raising a family is a high priority for this wise and witty team. If this is you: You're both on the same page almost all of the time—enjoy the smooth sailing!

Rabbit and Rat: These two signs make a good partnership for business or friendship, but not necessarily romance. Both tend to be self-centered, which spells disaster for a loving, sharing relationship. The Rabbit finds the Rat overbearing and distant. The Rat finds the Rabbit too disinterested. If this is you: You two might be able to work it out, but only if the Rat is not too intense and the Rabbit isn't very passive.

Rabbit and Ox: The silent and stubborn Ox irritates the Rabbit's gentle nature. The Rabbit wants a relationship to be easy, but the Ox's behavior causes friction. That means the Rabbit has to work very hard to make the relationship compatible. The Rabbit's nature is to run from distressing situations rather than to work through them. If this is you: You'll probably need outside help if you two plan on making this last for the long haul.

Rabbit and Monkey: The Monkey is a trickster—the Rabbit is on the up-and-up. The Rabbit cannot trust the Monkey, and the Monkey thinks the Rabbit is too prudent. Petty disagreements may turn into shouting matches, which will send the Rabbit packing. If this is you: You two are in for some difficult times unless the Monkey learns to be tolerant and Rabbit grows a thicker skin.

Rabbit and Rooster: These opposites do not attract. The Rooster is a hypercritical snob. The Rabbit is much too sensitive for the Rooster. The Rabbit is a steady, methodical worker; while the Rooster works in fits and spurts, indulging too often for the Rabbit's liking. To find true happiness together will be hard work, and it may be easier to find love elsewhere. If this is you: You two don't have fate's blessing! You're exact lunar opposites, and that will likely spell disaster.

Rabbit and Tiger: The Tiger is too brash, impulsive, and overbearing for the submissive Rabbit. Since the Rabbit will do anything to avoid confrontation, this pair appears doomed from the start. The Rabbit cringes when the Tiger roars and eventually tires of the constant racket. The Tiger knows just how to push the Rabbit's buttons and does so at every opportunity. If this is you: You two aren't going to have it easy. With a lot of effort you can probably make it work, but is it worth it?

Rabbit and Horse: The Horse is reckless and daring, ready to gallop off at a moment's notice. The Rabbit hangs back, not willing to take a chance. The Rabbit definitely does not like danger or exhibitionism, which is the Horse's pride and glory. For the Rabbit, life in this relationship is too chaotic. The Horse thinks the Rabbit is a drag. If this is you: You'll need plenty of outside assistance and a whole lot of love to keep this relationship from driving you both crazy.

 ## WRITTEN IN THE STARS

Celebrity unions are fairly easy to analyze when we see them in terms of the Chinese zodiac. Since most people are familiar with the players, let's see what went wrong with this couple.

Actress Anjelica Huston, born July 8, 1951, under the sign of the Rabbit, comes from a long line of Hollywood notables. Her father was John Huston, a well-respected director. She is best known for her role as Morticia Addams in the 1991 movie *The Addams Family* and its 1993 sequel, but she has appeared in dozens of movies.

In 1981, she costarred in a remake of *The Postman Always Rings Twice* with her longtime beau Jack Nicholson, born on April 22, 1937, under the sign of the Ox. Anjelica and Jack lived together from 1973 to 1989. They were considered to be one of Hollywood's most powerful couples for many years. But the Ox and the Rabbit are not compatible signs, so let's see what happened and why.

Jack Nicholson appears to exhibit all the qualities of the silent and stubborn Ox. He even looks like an Ox, at five-foot-nine and sturdily built, and he is known for his periodic outbursts. In 1994, in an apparent fit of rage, he smashed a man's car window with a golf club. This doesn't sound like someone that the gentle Rabbit could be with for the long run—although they did spend seventeen years together.

Rabbits like kids and Anjelica Huston is no exception. She was reported by *www.imdb.com* as saying: "I once wanted to have children, and it was not my choice not to have children, but it hasn't broken my heart that I haven't."

The Ox has a different agenda than the Rabbit, which means the Rabbit has to expend more energy than it's worth to make it work. Sometimes it is easier to cut one's losses and move on, and that's what Anjelica Huston did. In 1992 she married Robert Graham, Jr., and the five-foot-ten former model appears to have found happiness.

The Dynamic Dragon

Years of the Dragon: 1904, 1916, 1928, 1940, 1952, 1964, 1976, 1988, and 2000

Famous Dragons: Grace Kelly, Martin Luther King, Jr., Bruce Lee, Al Pacino, Vivica A. Fox, and Calista Flockhart

Season: Spring

Best qualities: Sentimental, astute, vivacious, successful, independent, purposeful, and perceptive

Worst qualities: Stubborn, difficult, irritable, loud, impulsive, and judgmental

THE DYNAMIC DRAGON'S PERSONALITY

The fearless Dragon rules! When a Dragon enters a room, heads turn. When a Dragon chairs a meeting, people listen. At home, there's no doubt that the Dragon is the boss.

Dragons like to win and they usually do. They are born leaders, and their limitless energy and constant motion are enough to make anyone who watches them want to take a nap. Their exuberance spills over into their voices, which are loud, and their gestures, which are grand (take Rev. Martin Luther King, Jr., and Al Pacino, for examples). In the Chinese culture, the Dragon is the symbol of power and wealth—a reputation well earned.

Dragons are charming, ambitious, successful, and grounded in the real world. They are deep thinkers and intellectuals who can trip over their supersized egos. Their eagerness tempers their self-importance, and they make loyal friends.

Dragons are monarchs, religious zealots, and corporate CEOs. They draw others into their schemes. It's hard to say "no" to Dragons, and they don't take kindly to it when you do. Dragons expect people to comply; and, when challenged, they don't hold back their opinions. Their motto is: "Let's do it MY way—or else."

Dragons speak truthfully—usually without considering other people's feelings. Being polite is not their forte, and Dragons don't take criticism well. When their buttons are pushed, they vent vociferously then simmer down to a slow boil. As the emotional storm blows over, Dragons put old issues behind them and move on to the future. The past is done and they let bygones by bygones. The present and the future are filled with promise, and they want to take full advantage. Of course, Dragons always expect to be forgiven for their thunderous outbursts, because they consider themselves the most wonderful of all God's creatures. They don't see themselves as others might: irritating, loud, impulsive, and boastful.

Always on a mission, Dragons are fearsome foes and wonderful allies. Without projects, plans, or missions, Dragons become restless and depressed. It's important to keep them busy at all times. They thrive on challenge.

HER HEART

The Dragoness is very self-assured—she dresses in the latest fashion and feels that good grooming is next to godliness. She has her eye on the social scene and loves to mingle with the "in" crowd. A lifestyle of the rich and famous is the shining star she yearns to attain. Given the lady Dragon's energetic and ambitious nature, the world is her oyster. You can almost hear her say: "I know what I want and I know how to get it."

The lady Dragon is determined to stay in shape. She manages to appear more youthful than she really is through exercise and proper nutrition. She carries herself well and wards off wrinkles with a steady diet of facials. This careful lady takes care to protect her delicate skin when out in the sun.

In addition to her physical appearance, the female Dragon is charming and mysterious. She has a stunning sense of humor and quick wit that make her equally appealing to both men and women. She is smart, too, and well respected in whatever profession she chooses. The lady Dragon cultivates her mind with higher educational degrees and literary material. She surrounds herself with fine art, good music, and lives in a stunning home.

The Dragoness believes men and women should be treated equally, and she's not shy about making this point when she observes a situation that discriminates. She is logical and pragmatic, but she does not like to be criticized—it makes her defensive and irritable. She will snap out of a bad mood when she is good and ready, and there is no pushing her to be reasonable on anybody else's time schedule.

Women born under this dynamic sign make excellent teachers, entrepreneurs, dietitians, professors, lawyers, and doctors. Raising children comes naturally. Organized and efficient, mindful of time and the things she needs to do each day, the lady Dragon does not waste time and resents when people pester her with trivial matters. For her, time is money.

 ## HIS HEART

Ruthless in business, the male Dragon is likely to be wealthy and powerful—two enticements for the fairer sex. He is generous with his money, although not to the extreme. He does not overspend, and he knows the value of a dollar. He is only free with money on special occasions.

The male Dragon is emotionally open—he does not hide his heart. With his direct no-nonsense approach, you'll know exactly what he's thinking. And when he wants to do something, like go on a trip or spend the day skydiving, he will expect you to hop to it. If you don't want to go, he'll be angry for a moment, then he'll find someone else to party with. The Dragon doesn't let anyone rain on his parade. As long as he's having fun, grudges are soon forgotten.

Moving through life at breakneck speed, the male Dragon does not tolerate laziness in anyone he employs. He knows that most people don't operate on his time schedule, but he wants everyone to challenge themselves, the way he does. Give him 110 percent and he's satisfied. He excels as a politician, a corporate CEO, an attorney, and in the field of entertainment. After all, he loves to be center stage.

The male Dragon sets an example of leadership by delegating—right down to the most menial task. He is not a micro-manager; but he expects that once an assignment is given, it will be completed to his satisfaction and on time. He says: "You don't ask, you don't get."

The male Dragon is always surprised when he is rejected by a lady. He thinks that he's the best suitor, the most charming companion, and the love of any woman's life. Often, his arrogance and pride are a turnoff, especially to the female Ox who finds him abrasive and quixotic— always running off on a whimsical adventure. If you want a steady stay-at-home guy who'll watch television, forget it. The male Dragon is on a mad dash to conquer the world.

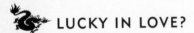 **LUCKY IN LOVE?**

Don't expect a lady Dragon to pine away for the love of a man. She is self-sufficient, content with her work, and happy to socialize with a wide variety of friends. She has numerous hobbies; but if a guy wants to wine and dine her, that's fine. If no guy is around, that's fine, too. She is not a clinging vine, nor does she believe her place is in the home.

If and when she does settle down, the female Dragon makes a terrific helpmate. She wants to be indulged now and then and appreciated at all times. She may even appear to be a spoiled princess, but she has a good heart. And even if she won't get her nails dirty planting a garden, she is a vivacious storyteller and a lusty lover. The lady Dragon comes on strong; she's not shy—her mouth is uncensored, and she is opinionated and feisty.

Men pursue her relentlessly, and she falls in "like" easily. She tests a man's mettle with her brash opinions and weeds out those worth pursuing. The female Dragon is the one who usually breaks off a romance; but once she meets that special guy, she will quickly settle down to a passion-filled life as long as he accepts her headstrong attitude.

It's easy to fall for a male Dragon—his confidence, self-assurance, and charm draw women into his aura. He may marry early in life. If not, he will be perfectly content as a bachelor. If Dragons and their mates split up, they immerse themselves in their work or in a cause that keeps them energized and operating toward a positive goal.

Beware, for marriage is not usually on the male Dragon's agenda. And if he does marry, it's for the convenience and not necessarily because he's wild crazy in love. When he does declare his love, it is genuine and straight from the heart. Remember, he minces no words.

Verbal skirmishes are a daily part of life with a male Dragon. He can always find some small issue that needs addressing. If his fault-finding is nipped in the bud, the Dragon guy is a fine partner.

 ## FOR BETTER OR WORSE

Dragon and Rat: This is an awesome twosome with plenty of positive energy and a lively spirit. The Dragon is strong, and the Rat is clever. Both are generous. The Rat is affectionate, and the Dragon is protective. With so much in common, this pair has the ability to make it work for better or worse. If this is you: You two are so well matched that your only problem would be not nipping small issues in the bud early on—so long as you take care of those, you'll do fine.

Dragon and Rabbit: The Rabbit admires the Dragon's leadership, and the Dragon appreciates the Rabbit's sympathy when things go awry. The Rabbit listens to the Dragon's complaints without judgment. As long as the

Dragon is careful not to aim his or her tirades at the Rabbit, all is well. If this is you: Be mindful of how you talk to one another, for your love is true and deep.

Dragon and Dragon: This is a powerhouse team. Each is capable and assertive in his or her own right. Together they form a pillar of strength. They can convert even the most soulless sinner or talk a vagrant into buying the Brooklyn Bridge. Their whirlwind life leaves others breathless, but they can burn and crash by running at too frantic a pace. If this is you: You two are fools to miss out on each other because you're so busy running around the world. Take some time to be quiet together, and enjoy your relationship or it may get swallowed up in the chaos you both create.

Dragon and Snake: The Snake admires the Dragon's ambition and success and makes an energetic helpmate. The same can be said of the Dragon. Intelligent and non-emotional, these two powerful signs complement each other; and if they work together toward a common goal, they make a commanding and highly charged romantic pair. If this is you: Enjoy each other and don't sweat the small stuff. Together you can overcome all obstacles.

Dragon and Horse: The Horse's independence goes hand in hand with the Dragon's wild ambition. Both are leaders; and as long as they are not treading on each other's toes or territory, there will be peace. There is plenty of passion with this pair. If this is you: You two are bound to do great things together just as long as you remember to keep a dialogue going at all times.

Dragon and Monkey: The Dragon is drawn to the irrepressible Monkey, and the Monkey is awed by the Dragon's incredibly positive spirit. They are both clever, and they can hatch up so many schemes there is no way to pull them all off. If they can decide on one and work together, it will surely be a success. If this is you: You two know the benefits of scheming, but do you remember the pleasure of staying in? Too often you two forget about going to bed, which is too bad, because there's a lot of passion between you.

Dragon and Ox: This borderline couple will struggle for power. The Ox is stubborn and the Dragon is pushy. Although the partners may agree that one will rule the roost, verbal contracts between lovers are blown apart when emotions are involved. Since the Ox holds back and the Dragon lets loose, the emotional balance is lopsided. When they work as one, they are unstoppable. If this is you: You'll both need to keep in mind that communication is key. Get yourselves some outside help, and you just might be able to make the relationship work.

Dragon and Tiger: The Dragon and the Tiger are a colorful, dynamic, and flamboyant couple. They're social butterflies, and everyone around them thinks, "Wow, what a pair." The Dragon needs to be in control at all times, and the Tiger chafes at taking the back seat. If this is you:

You two need to compromise and keep communication open and honest or the tension will become unbearable.

Dragon and Sheep: This union may actually work out since the Dragon feels protective toward the Sheep and the Sheep lets the Dragon do his or own thing. The Sheep is content to stay at home while the Dragon seeks excitement. When they are together, they are respectful of each other's personality. As long as the Sheep doesn't whine and the Dragon doesn't breathe fire, they stand a chance of making a long-lasting commitment. If this is you: You have a lot going for you, despite your differences. Remember to give each other some room to breathe.

Dragon and Rooster: There are possibilities for this pair, since there is mutual admiration. Both want success and respect. To make it work, the Rooster should be careful not to henpeck the Dragon over every little detail. In return, the Dragon might want to tone down the ego just a bit. With their personalities more tempered and less abrasive, this couple can make a long-lasting commitment. If this is you: It's always better to concentrate on the positive and not dwell on the negative aspects of your relationship to make it smooth sailing.

Dragon and Dog: This poor combination of personalities will likely clash. The Dragon is too overbearing for the trusting and quiet Dog. The Dog wants to be treated equally, but the Dragon will have no part of it. A Dragon's superior attitude annoys the Dog to no end—the Dog will nip and cause the Dragon to bellow. If this is you: You two need to find a middle ground of peaceful coexistence or go your separate ways—if you ignore your issues, the situation will become too stressful.

Dragon and Pig: The flashy Dragon may be too overbearing for the conservative Pig. The Dragon's need to be right doesn't bother the Pig, but it gets to be a drag after a while and eventually grates like a rasp. There could be plenty of good times together and only a few serious conflicts if each accepts the personality of the other. If this is you: You should try walking in your partner's shoes before rushing to judgment. If you cannot get along, seek outside help.

 WRITTEN IN THE STARS

Celebrity unions are fairly easy to analyze when we see them in terms of the Chinese zodiac. Since most people are familiar with the players, let's see what's up with this unusual couple.

If you want to see a Dragon in action, look no further than Al Pacino. Born April 25, 1940, Pacino—a Dragon—is one of the most respected and gifted actors in America today with a string of hit movies, each one showcasing his amazing talent. He played a gritty cop in *Serpico* and received Academy Award nominations for *The Godfather*, . . . *And Justice for All, Dick Tracy,* and *Glengarry Glen Ross*. His famous dark, owl eyes and gravelly, hoarse voice make him instantly recognizable and brought him the coveted Best Actor award for his mesmerizing performance as a blind ex-military officer in *Scent of a Woman* in 1992.

He is known as one of Hollywood's most tried and true bachelors. He has a daughter with former girlfriend Jan Tarrant, and he had a longtime romance with *Godfather* costar Diane Keaton. Most recently, he has been committed to Beverly D'Angelo, with whom he has twins Anton and Olivia, born January 25, 2001.

Beverly D'Angelo was born on November 15, 1954, under the sign of the Horse. She has more than sixty acting credits. The petite blonde is best known for her role as Ellen Griswold in the *National Lampoon's Vacation* series. She also played country singer Patsy Cline in *Coal Miner's Daughter* in 1980.

Pacino and D'Angelo share responsibilities for their tiny twins although they are not married. They are a compatible pair—the Horse is independent and the Dragon is ambitious. Both are leaders; and as long as they are not treading on each other's toes or territory, there will be peace. The key to their success is keeping a dialogue going at all times. There is plenty of passion with this pair, but obviously the Dragon does not want to make this a more permanent union. And, in fact, they keep separate households. The beauty of the free-spirited Horse and the power-driven Dragon is that each is content with the way things are.

The Prudent Snake

Years of the Snake: 1905, 1917, 1929, 1941, 1953, 1965, 1977, 1989, and 2001

Famous Snakes: Howard Hughes, Henry Fonda, John F. Kennedy, Dean Martin, Oprah Winfrey, Courteney Cox, and Brooke Shields

Season: Spring

Best qualities: Rational, cultured, brainy, wise, intuitive, funny, sympathetic, gracious, relaxed, and determined

Worst qualities: Parsimonious, cheap, rash, spiteful, indolent, secretive, crotchety, cold, and calculating

THE PRUDENT SNAKE'S PERSONALITY

In the West, we think of snakes as slithery, unsavory people who use deception to get what they want. In the East, however, and especially in Chinese astrology, this is not the case. The Snake's personality is closely linked to the Dragon, but less flashy and more intuitive. Think of the actor as the Dragon and the agent as the Snake, gathering information to make the best deals.

Snakes are the deepest thinkers of all the twelve signs in the Chinese zodiac. Endowed with innate wisdom, Snakes know and see all but do not tell all. Snakes like to operate in their own private worlds, communicating as little as possible with others. That's why they have a reputation of being cool and detached.

Snakes are considered the guardians of the treasure and, as such, want to live well—dining on fine food, going to plays and other cultural events. Snakes are soft-spoken and polite. They do not seek the limelight. Instead, Snakes stay in the corner observing the shenanigans and storing the information for a later date. Snakes rarely act out or cause a scene. They dress well and have excellent manners.

Unlike the Dragon, who spends money freely, the Snake is parsimonious—cheap, really. Snakes will indulge in a lavish meal, spending plenty on fine wines . . . but then leave a miserly tip. Since Snakes don't like to part with cash, they are frustrated that it costs money to have nice things. Their favorite expression is: "I think I can get a deal on this." To their credit, they have substantial bank accounts and rarely go broke.

Snakes want to look their best at all times and will do whatever it takes—like shedding their skin. Snakes take special care with their body; and although they may hesitate for a moment about plastic surgery or cosmetic dentistry—because these procedures are pricey—vanity wins out, and they give in. They justify the expense by saying: "There's nothing wrong with looking good."

Some scholars suggest that Snakes are liars. This is a broad generalization that does not hold true for every Snake on the planet. The habit of being secretive and noncommunicative leads to the conclusion that they are not telling the truth.

While Snakes can be quite charming, too often they begin to believe they are better than everyone else. They boost their fragile egos by stretching the truth—like the size of the one that got away—to make themselves appear grander than they really are. They need someone to bolster their sagging spirits when life doesn't go as planned or simply to adore and admire them. Snakes sometimes fail to live up to their own high expectations; and since they don't like losing, they can be downright rude when they get the short end of the stick.

On those occasions when life is less than perfect, Snakes may turn to alcohol or drugs, or they may stray from their mate in a desperate bid to feel needed. They find rejection devastating.

Order and sameness of routine appeal to the haughty Snake. They feel at home with a circle of familiar friends, with coworkers with whom they have worked for a long time, and in the home—which they may live in for most of their lives. They do not tolerate change well. Some Snakes will walk in the door and notice that their mate has moved a few objects around—like plants or the couch, for instance—and within minutes, everything is back where it was when they left that morning. Snakes are so set in their ways, they will stay in a marriage that isn't working and try to make the best of a bad situation.

HER HEART

Give the female Snake a credit card and she's a happy camper—as long as it's not her own greenbacks she's spending. The only thing she'd like better is a day at the spa. The lady Snake wants to look and feel her best—at all cost. That includes manicures, pedicures, makeovers, and cosmetic surgery, if she wants it. She keeps the hairdresser busy as she changes her appearance every few months.

The Snake can change her clothes five times a day—including undergarments, jewelry, and shoes. This small vanity makes her happy; and it doesn't hurt anyone, so you should try to accept her eccentricity with good graces.

The inner wisdom of the Snake gives her the gift of a sixth sense. She is a natural-born psychic; and with her ear to the ground, she knows all. Ask her, but she won't tell. Not all Snakes acknowledge this innate talent. Some may even deny it. But it's a part of their natures, and their expertise will eventually express itself in the right situation—to everyone's amazement, especially theirs.

Constantly in search of knowledge, the lady Snake can reinvent herself many times. She is a work in progress, and her unique sense of humor makes her fun to be around. Raising a family is not a top priority; but when she has kids, she does not spoil them. Instead, she expects them to grow up quickly and will delegate chores for them so they understand that life is not a free ride.

Lady Snakes have high standards for their mates. They aren't desperate and they won't settle. Female Snakes are mysterious, seductive, and intriguing—men clamor for their attention. Lady Snakes know how to use cosmetics and clothing to make themselves shine. They are ardent lovers and like the excitement of romance. Once committed, they will settle into partnerships with ease.

🐍 HIS HEART

He could charm the pocket off a kangaroo. But beware, the male Snake is tenacious in business or love. He can put the squeeze on you like a python or bite your head off. He is spiteful when crossed, and he may plot a fitting revenge.

The male Snake is debonair and meticulous about his appearance; he is drawn to designer labels. He may go overboard with his choice of clothing and on occasion will appear out of place, but this is his eccentricity and it does not reflect poorly on his character. Whenever the occasion arises, such as a backyard picnic or a trip to the beach, he will strip off his shirt and show off his body—his gift to the ladies.

Peaceful coexistence is the male Snake's ultimate goal. He does not care for danger or confrontation—though he will not shy away from it. To ensure this kind of placid, trouble-free existence, he will examine any situation for possible conflict. If he senses tension, he will either smooth things over or slither away. He wants to live without agitation or confusion. Because of this tendency to retreat in the face of turmoil, he has the reputation of being lazy or cowardly. That isn't true. The male Snake simply prefers to relax in his armchair or philosophize about the state of the world. In other words, these brainy characters intellectualize about everything and will talk about the human condition with anyone who will listen. Whether he is college educated or not, he is curious about many things; and curling up with a book, magazine article, or newspaper is high on his list of priorities. Male Snakes make excellent teachers, professors, therapists, researchers, detectives, and scientists. Male Snakes are unbiased mediators who try to treat others fairly and give each side a chance to make their point.

Male Snakes have a secretive side. When they feel pressured, communication ceases. Their tight-lipped attitude can be discouraging for a partner who doesn't understand that it is part of their nature.

When it comes to spending, the male Snake is tight with money. Despite this slight character flaw, he is popular with the ladies because he accepts people as they are—without trying to change them. This trait is especially appealing to women, who feel embraced by his straightforward attitude. But take heed, gals, he is a Casanova at heart and will slither from bed to bed without guilt or remorse.

🐍 LUCKY IN LOVE?

Female Snakes are known femme fatales. They look good, and they know it. This brazen attitude lures men to their side. Men swoon at their feet; and although female Snakes act cool, they're secretly thriving on the attention. Female Snakes love to be in love; it keeps them energized. Without it, they curl up and become withdrawn and introspective. It may take some prodding by well-meaning pals to get them back into the social scene after the end of an affair. And female Snakes have many affairs—before they finally settle down.

The way to a female Snake's heart is through pampering—wine and dine her and buy her an expensive gift, perhaps something that sparkles. Once she's hooked, she will look deep within your heart and soul. If she intuits that you are honest and sincere, you may get a second date with this fair-minded and brainy beauty.

Be forewarned, the lady Snake is not easy to live with. Despite their outward appearance of bravado, female Snakes lack self-assurance. She is a great mom and an attentive wife, however. Give her a kind word, a compliment, or a hug for the encouragement she needs to get through the day. If you don't, the lady Snake may seek comfort in the arms of another—she needs to know she is lovable or she'll curl up and withdraw.

The male Snake is a sexy beast—but remember, he is

also a shameless flirt and seducer. He considers himself an accomplished lover but his ultimate desire is not his own satisfaction—it's his partner's. The male Snake loves making love and feels that by bedding many women, he is doing the world a service. He doesn't see why anyone would be bothered by this altruistic attitude.

It is possible to bring a male Snake to his knees. Once wed, they make attentive husbands and caring dads. That does not mean his eyes will stop wandering. You can always spot a male Snake when you're out in public because he's ogling the pretty ladies. He'll tell you: "Don't be so insecure, I only have eyes for you!"

Oh, boy, he has that line down pat.

While he tries hard to be a faithful husband, it's not in his nature. If a male Snake strays, he will scoff it off as "no big deal." But a woman with a male Snake should not take it personally. He is not looking to slink out of the relationship and will probably stay, unless he's booted out.

FOR BETTER OR WORSE

Snake and Rat: Both want success. Both admire power. The Snake is smart, and the Rat is imaginative. When one says "time to stop" the other would do well to listen. In business and in bed, this couple is compatible. If this is you: You two have a great shot of making it—as long as you are mindful of each other's opinions.

Snake and Ox: The Snake likes the fortitude of the dependable Ox. The Ox is patient and rational and prevents the Snake from taking absurd risks. The Snake appreciates the Ox's logic and steadfastness and is willing to work long and hard to please the Ox. The Ox returns the favor with unassuming diligence. If this is you: You're a compatible pair who can be successful in love and business.

Snake and Rabbit: There's no real chemistry between these two, but that doesn't mean it can't work. The Snake needs constant reassurance that everything is okay, but the Rabbit's detachment may cause the Snake some concern. The same happens the other way around—which keeps them both guessing about the relationship and trying to please one another. While the passion between them is lacking, they have an enduring friendship. If this is you: You shouldn't expect fireworks. Instead, enjoy the slow simmer of mutual respect and admiration.

Snake and Dragon: Each brings respect and admiration to the relationship, which makes this a compatible pair. Both are ambitious; and with the Dragon in front and the Snake bringing up the rear, they can accomplish whatever they want. They work in sync, and altercations are few and far between. When there is a dispute, it's settled quickly. These two know how to kiss and make up—with passion. If this is you: You two were made for each other—there's no doubt you're kindred spirits.

Snake and Snake: Not all like-minded signs can get along, but two Snakes can. Since they are so similar in spirit, they don't need to talk. Each knows what the other is thinking.

Their basic problem is that they are not always on the same track and there is a lack of communication. Since neither is a big talker, they must be careful not to let bad feelings fester without dealing with the issues. If this is you: You two are stable without being boring—you're friends and lovers, and life couldn't be better—as long as you keep the lines of communication open.

Snake and Rooster: Fiercely competitive and completely outspoken, the Rooster brings out the best in the Snake. From morning to night, the Rooster prods the Snake into utilizing every talent. The Rooster has so much going on, there is no time to obsess about what's on the Snake's mind. With both working toward a common goal, this is a fruitful union—even if the Rooster does get peeved now and then about the Snake's slacking. If this is you: The zest you use for making oodles of money spills over into the bedroom, where passion sizzles.

Snake and Tiger: The Tiger is aggressive and wants to run the show. The Snake does not take orders well and feels unappreciated. The outspoken Tiger will have the Snake scurrying for cover when a crisis arises; and because the balance of power is lopsided, communication is very poor. If this is you: If you both don't make a concerted effort to overcome your basic differences, the prospect of a long-term union is not good.

Snake and Horse: The Horse is energetic and passionate, the Snake is slower moving and distant. How could these two find common ground? The Horse wants to know what the Snake is feeling but will not have much luck finding out. The Snake will find the Horse too hyper and overbearing. Whether they can change their basic nature to make it work is anyone's guess. If this is you: You may not have what it takes to run the distance; but if you truly care about one another, you will make every effort, even counseling.

Snake and Sheep: The ambitious, intellectual Snake is no match for the affable, earthy Sheep. The Sheep's neediness will grate on the Snake's nerves, and the Sheep will feel slighted by the Snake's lack of compassion. They may stay together for the sake of the children because the Snake doesn't want to leave and the Sheep is fearful of being alone. They may wait until the nest is empty, then go separate ways. If this is you: You may be happier as friends or business partners than lovers. Better to move on if you're miserable.

Snake and Monkey: The outgoing Monkey cannot trust the silent Snake; and, likewise, the Snake feels the Monkey is too clever. With a lack of trust, both will be too nervous to relax, which does not bode well for this union. If this is you: You two will never agree to compromise— but if you do, the relationship may have a shot.

Snake and Dog: These signs are on nearly the exact opposite sides of the zodiac. The Snake and the Dog will have problems—even if there is an initial attraction. Both are smart and ambitious, both enjoy the comfort of home and a circle of close friends. Neither likes change; and while they have a lot in common, it may be too much for their own good. If this is you: You'll find this relationship is as bumpy as they come—if you're really serious, seek counseling.

Snake and Pig: These two don't have much in common. The Pig likes to party, the Snake does not. The Pig is downright honest, the Snake is a little less so. The Pig is generous to a fault, the Snake is stingy. If this is you: This union can only work with a lot of effort!

🐍 WRITTEN IN THE STARS

Celebrity unions are fairly easy to analyze when we see them in terms of the Chinese zodiac. Since most people are familiar with the players, let's see if this well-known couple will last for the long haul.

Talk show host Oprah Winfrey was born on January 29, 1954, under the sign of the Snake. Over the past two decades, she has carved out a career as the queen of daytime television. Throughout her career, Oprah has used her innate wisdom and intelligence to create a name for herself. Today she is so well known and respected that when she talks, people listen.

Oprah has been romantically involved with businessman Stedman Graham since 1986—but the two have no plans to marry. Graham, born March 6, 1951, is a Rabbit.

In an interview with Gwen Gill of the *Sunday Times* (a popular newspaper in South Africa), Oprah said: "I am a woman of independent means. . . . The only thing that would make me get married is to have children, but it looks like my eggs are old now, so that won't happen."

According to the Chinese zodiac, this pair is destined to have plenty of ups and downs. The Snake is not always forthcoming with compliments and can be cool and detached. Female Snakes like the high life; they like to be seen. Rabbits, on the other hand, are shy and don't care to be in the limelight. This point is illustrated in the fact that Ms. Winfrey is photographed at numerous gala events without Stedman Graham at her side.

As a Rabbit, Stedman may feel he is carrying the entire weight of the relationship on his shoulders. Rabbits also need assurance that all is well. While Oprah builds an empire and attends to her many obligations as an actress, producer, and television personality, the Rabbit may feel left out in the cold. However, with mutual respect and support, this can be an enduring and fruitful union.

The Sociable Horse

Years of the Horse: 1906, 1918, 1930, 1942, 1954, 1966, 1978, 1990, and 2002

Famous Horses: Thomas Edison, John Travolta, Barbra Streisand, Joanne Woodward, Sean Connery, David Schwimmer, and Paul McCartney

Season: Summer

Best qualities: Friendly, well-spoken, self-assured, smart, athletic, bewitching, independent, industrious, and sensual

Worst qualities: Egotistical, selfish, hotheaded, defiant, impatient, unsympathetic, and blunt

![horse icon] THE SOCIABLE HORSE'S PERSONALITY

The Horse in the Chinese zodiac exhibits the same characteristics as the Western sign Gemini—a dual personality and changeable emotions. One minute Horses are cheerful and upbeat, and in the next they are stubborn and angry. But, overall, Horses are spirited, engaging people who are easy to get along with. They know where they want to go with their lives and careers, and they have the stamina to get there.

Athletics are important to most Horses. They tend to be swift, graceful, agile, and strong. Sports that involve endurance, such as marathon running, speed skating, downhill skiing, inline skating, or long-distance bicycling, appeal to their free-spirited nature. You won't find Horses cooped up unless the weather is inclement. When Horses can't find the time or place to exercise, they begin to chafe and become irritable. Blowing off their energy through physical activity relieves the stress of their daily lives.

The Horse has an explosive spirit and a raging temper, which bursts forth but then quickly subsides. This brashness works to the detriment of the otherwise sociable Horse because most people don't want to spend time around someone who has erratic outbursts or who yells when easily provoked—certainly not the Rabbit or the Sheep!

Horses demand a great deal from friends, family, and lovers. They think they are the cat's meow; and when their needs aren't satisfied, all hell breaks loose. They tend to be impatient, selfish, and unmindful of other people's feelings. Although they know better, Horses often bark orders without remembering to say "please" and "thank you."

Horses have above average intelligence, and they are gifted with amazing powers of persuasion. They can talk the tuxedo off a penguin. Convincing others comes naturally. That's why the Horse is a smooth operator—in the boardroom and in the bedroom. It's hard to say "no" to a relentless Horse—they are hard to resist.

Part of their allure is the confidence they project. As natural-born leaders, they wait impatiently for others to catch up. Their minds race a million miles a minute, and anyone who lags behind mentally or physically will be left in their dust. This tendency toward frustration makes it difficult for them to be mentors or teachers—they are simply too high-strung. "Get with the program" is their favorite expression.

Horses are generous with money, but stingy with time—they never have enough of it to get everything done. Horses in positions of authority, including with their own offspring, do not like to repeat themselves. They like to give directions once, and they expect their underlings to "get it."

In business, Horses are self-starters and go-getters. They're hot to trot, so to speak. They operate by setting goals and achieving them quickly and efficiently. They are not like Dragons, who always have a new plan or scheme. Horses see an opportunity and go for it with blinders on. Horses are incredible when obstacles arise—they will not be dissuaded. Hold a Horse back, and you'll see a nervous Nellie, champing at the bit.

 **HER HEART**

The female Horse is her own person. She's not seductive like the Snake or an amiable homemaker like the Ox. This lady is self-assured and socially adept. She walks into a room with her shoulders back and her head high. The Mare dresses elegantly in classic clothing, and she usually handles herself gracefully. But under stress, she becomes moody and agitated.

The female Horse cannot abide being idle. She is forever on the move, juggling career, kids, spouse, and social obligations. When someone tries to rein her in or when she falls ill, she becomes irritated and short-tempered. She hates being sick since it interferes with her routine.

Once her mind is made up, the Mare has the strength and determination to finish any project she starts. She is courageous and fearless, and she thrives on challenge. "Think positively" is her motto. She doesn't believe in failure. Any career is open to the lady Horse—from the arts to medicine, and teaching to police detective work. A regular sit-down job is not ideal because she needs more to feel satisfied.

Life with a Mare isn't fun and games all of the time—she can be controlling and bossy. The lady Horse wants things done her way and on her schedule. When she is under pressure, she acts temperamental and expects others to cater to her smallest whims. The Mare is blunt to a fault—she never hesitates to share her harsh judgments of other people's character.

The Mare could use a better sense of humor, a little

less ego; and she could be more down to earth. But she's an honest, forthright, and upbeat friend and an ardent lover. Despite her abrasive qualities, whatever she does, she does well.

 ## HIS HEART

Ever see a man walk into a room, snap his fingers, and suddenly be surrounded by a flock of beauties? That's a male Horse. Confident, arrogant, surefooted, filled with energy and the promise of a good time in the sack, the Horse is a gifted babe magnet.

Woe to the woman who thinks she can tame this strong-willed hero. He marches to his own beat and comes and goes as he pleases. Don't try to rope him into a routine—he'll break free and gallop away.

To communicate effectively with a male Horse, be blunt. Some women have a way of talking in circles before getting to the punch line, or they become emotional when they have an issue to address. The male Horse can't stand when people use circular logic or emotion when talking. He's a linear thinker who is only interested in the punch line. "Spit it out!" is his favorite expression. If you are forcefully direct, he will respect you more than if you try to run mental rings around him.

Horses make excellent politicians, salesmen, and athletes since they can go the distance without anyone outdoing them. That's the challenge they set up for themselves. Winning is their main goal; and they'll do whatever it takes to cross the finish line, to get the account, or to get the woman. The only thing that sometimes gets in the way is their huge egos. When that happens, the Horse comes across as an insufferable boor, but he doesn't care. He's running his own race, and he's going to win, come hell or high water.

The male Horse sets the rules, and he expects others to obey—including his employees and his kids. He needs respect and demands it from those around him.

Many male Horses are obsessed with sex. Strip clubs, X-rated movies—even paying for intimate relations—are part of their natures. They may even frequent strip clubs while they're in committed relationships. They're swash-bucklers at heart—but those women don't mean anything to him. When a male Horse falls in love—he's yours completely.

LUCKY IN LOVE?

The female Horse's heart is as whimsical and fickle as she is. She tends to attract men who are not as intelligent or driven as she is, thus she feels superior—and her guy feels like a flunkey. Ironically, when the relationship sours, the female Horse is shocked and can't figure out what went wrong. Or, she'll find a guy who doesn't want to work as hard as she does and it really bothers her. "Why should I be pulling all the weight?" she asks. Ideally, the Mare needs a strong, determined, powerful mate—someone who wants a headstrong woman to boost his career (perhaps a Dragon or Tiger) or simply a guy who believes that a powerful woman is an asset.

The female Horse is a sensual and passionate lover who may be skittish at first. Although she is a faithful partner, when things are not going perfectly, she may stray—until the guilt sets in. Once she is home, she's remorseful and moody until her guilt subsides. But before long, she is back in form, raring to go and as lusty as ever.

The male Horse shows affection by bestowing gifts, so don't expect him to gush romantic platitudes. When he loves a woman, he doesn't feel the need to express it. He believes that his actions speak louder than any words possibly could—and, in this case, he's right. The male Horse is a fickle character—loving one woman after another—without a long-term commitment. This super stud thrives on short, passionate affairs—they are notches in his saddle. If your male Horse strays, take matters into your own hands—be irresistible to him. Look appealing, challenge him intellectually, and make him work hard to win you back.

Trying to reach his emotional core is a lesson in futility; so is getting him to talk about his problems. Either coax him into romance with good humor and great appreciation or get out of the relationship.

 ## FOR BETTER OR WORSE

Horse and Tiger: This couple is the dynamic duo. The Tiger is bold and the Horse is resourceful and full of energy. How could this team lose? Both are passionate, industrious extroverts. They mesmerize others with their lively and carefree spirit. And they fascinate each other in bed with their zest for living and loving. If this is you: You have everything going for you—consider yourselves blessed.

Horse and Dragon: This dynamic pair makes things happen. The Dragon's power combined with the Horse's speed creates an unbeatable business team. When struggles for dominance take place, their good communication skills come in handy for resolving differences. A mutual respect and passion for life give these two a solid foundation. These two love to travel to exotic places where they immerse themselves in other cultures and customs. If this is you: You are soul mates, so consider yourselves two of the lucky ones and iron out small differences quickly so they don't disrupt the love that flows between you.

Horse and Horse: These two lively, spirited people have a relationship that shines with positive energy. Neither of them is jealous or petty. They are independent and have their own interests. Since both have mood swings, they learn to get out of each other's way to keep the peace. If this is you: You two should give each other some space when you're feeling irritable. Make sure you plan plenty of activities you can do together.

Horse and Sheep: The gentle Sheep is a good mate for the quick-witted Horse. The Sheep is content to follow the Horse, which suits the Horse just fine. The steadfast Sheep complements the changeable Horse. Both have a good sense of humor, which keeps small problems from becoming major issues; and when the Horse gets snippy with the Sheep, peace is restored with an apology and a gift from the heart. If this is you: You both know how to avoid major conflicts by using good common sense. Bravo for you!

Horse and Monkey: The mutual admiration these two share may work to their benefit—or not. With both the quick-witted Horse and the clever Monkey working toward a common goal, nothing can get in their way—except themselves. They are both selfish to some degree, and they may be too smart for their own good. If this is you: You two are a good team with problems. But don't fret— with plenty of communication and love, you can resolve your differences.

Horse and Dog: Both the Horse and Dog are smart, eager, and willing to work hard. They are practical and loyal. In fact, the usually wayward Horse appears happy to settle down with the accepting Dog. If this is you: You two probably don't need a book to tell you your soul mates—it's been obvious since you laid eyes on one another.

Horse and Rat: The Rat is a homebody who wants a partner that will share domestic chores and responsibility. Unfortunately, the Horse's independence and love of freedom take precedence over home life. The cynical Rat and the selfish Horse will quickly get on each other's nerves and bring out the worst in the other. If this is you: You two opposites will both need to compromise a lot, and you'll probably have to seek outside help if you really want this relationship to work.

Horse and Ox: The Ox is rigid, stubborn, and conventional. The Horse is spirited, unconventional, and also stubborn. The Ox is cautious and prudent, and the Horse is spontaneous. This poor mix of personalities will lead to conflict, and both parties should agree to work on their differences for a better partnership. If this is you: Because of your basic animal nature, it may seem that you are struggling against the current. You may have to let go in order to go with the flow.

Horse and Rabbit: The Horse and Rabbit would get along fine were it not for the Horse's temper. When the Horse is sweet-natured, all is well. Then the explosion rocks the Rabbit's world and wrecks everything. The Rabbit will not be able to take the Horse's up-and-down nature for very long before becoming sullen and withdrawn—this response will exasperate the Horse even more. The Rabbit needs to learn not to take the Horse's ranting personally. If this is you: Your relationship is rocky, but it has potential. You two need to determine a plan for dealing with the Horse's temper—if you're successful at cooling it down, everything else should be a breeze.

Horse and Snake: This is not a lovey-dovey couple. The cool Snake is hypocritical of the Horse's rambunctious nature. The Horse wants to get the show on the road, but the Snake has slithered into a corner to brood. The Horse is impatient, and this leads to problems. The introverted Snake is no match for the extroverted Horse. If this is you: You're in for a rough ride unless you turn to counseling and you both commit to doing the work.

Horse and Rooster: The Rooster is critical, but the Horse isn't concerned with details and does not like to be criticized. Both reek of self-confidence and want to be in charge. Something has to give, and it's usually the Horse, who will gallop off, leaving the Rooster to pick away at someone else. If this is you: You're both going to have to compromise or forget it—life's too short to waste time being so miserable.

Horse and Pig: The slow-moving Pig will drive the nimble Horse nutty. If the Pig is well off financially, the Horse may stay to enjoy the ride. But it will be a bumpy one. However, if they have independent hobbies and interests and a group of mutual friends, it could work out for the long run. If this is you: You two may be able to make this work, but not without some effort.

WRITTEN IN THE STARS

Celebrity unions are fairly easy to analyze when we see them in terms of the Chinese zodiac. Since most people are familiar with the players, let's see why this famous show-biz couple gets along.

Superstar John Travolta from Englewood, N.J., was born on February 18, 1954, under the sign of the Horse.

The Horse is spirited and gallant, headstrong and hard-working. Travolta fits that description to a tee. Just think about him in the movie *Grease*; now there's a Horse man! Off screen, he had his share of love affairs, but not as many as one would think for such a good-looking, talented guy, until he settled down and became a family man.

In 1991, Travolta married actress Kelly Preston, who was born in Honolulu, Hawaii on October 13, 1962, under the sign of the Tiger.

According to the Chinese zodiac, this is a win-win situation, and it shows. In their ten years together, they have produced two lovely kids, Jett and Ella Bleu. The Tiger is bold, and the Horse is resourceful and full of energy. This team can't lose. Both are passionate, industrious extroverts. They mesmerize others with their lively and carefree spirit. Nothing gets between these two and their ongoing projects.

In this harmonious union, each brings out the best in the other. Preston gives her strong-willed hero husband plenty of room to gallop—or fly in this case, for Travolta is a crackerjack pilot. Even though Horse men can be blunt and hotheaded, they are also sweet-tempered, kind-hearted, and jolly souls. Travolta is known in Hollywood to be one of the nicest guys around.

The Shy Sheep

Years of the Sheep: 1907, 1919, 1931, 1943, 1955, 1967, 1979, 1991, and 2003

Famous Sheep: Barbara Walters, Sir Laurence Olivier, Matt LeBlanc, Pamela Anderson, and Bruce Willis

Season: Summer

Best qualities: Creative, smart, gracious, inventive, lovable, determined, romantic, peace-loving, and giving

Worst qualities: Pessimistic, unhappy, disorganized, careless, unreliable, late, weak, and helpless

THE SHY SHEEP'S PERSONALITY

Mild-mannered, even bashful, Sheep are gentle souls known for their compassion and their giving nature. They champion the rights of those less fortunate and always root for the underdog.

Generous with emotions and money, Sheep will offer you a place to stay, food to eat, and even the wool off their backs. Sheep symbolize prosperity and comfort—they know that whatever is given will come back tenfold. The Sheep's favorite expression is: "What goes around, comes around."

Working on a project of any kind with a Sheep will be a pleasure because this hard-working individual pulls his or her own weight, and then some.

The Sheep is lucky in love and with finances. Money seems to find its way into the Sheep's pocket, through hard work, good fortune, or receiving an inheritance.

Sheep have glib tongues and can get what's needed without harsh words or temper tantrums. They say, "You can catch more bees with honey than with vinegar." Like Rabbits, Sheep avoid confrontation whenever possible and would rather sulk than fight. In the long run, Sheep prevail in getting what they want through quiet determination. Sheep can be pushed very far before they push back. But when they do push back, watch out. Sheep have powerful friends and know that the pen is mightier than the sword.

Sheep don't come right out and say what's on their minds. They make others pry it out of them. They'll "bleat" around the bush while secret hurts stay buried deep within until someone cares to ask. Sheep do well with counseling or therapy to rid themselves of these bad feelings, which stunt their emotional growth.

Count on the caring Sheep to remember birthdays, anniversaries, and other important dates. They keep a calendar in their heads, but they also jot down things that they want to remember, for they have a lot on their minds. Sheep take it personally when someone close to their heart forgets their special day. If you have a friend, lover, or relative who is a Sheep, make sure to call or send a card.

Sheep are optimists at heart, and yet worries creep in to sabotage their good feelings—they should stay away from bad news on television and in the newspaper. The sensitive soul of the loyal Sheep will take those troubles as their own and fret about them for days. Sheep should avoid violent movies, which upset them; however, they enjoy documentaries and romantic comedies.

Sheep are followers. They like being part of the team because it protects them from incurring criticism for making poor decisions. When things go wrong, they can say that it wasn't their fault—it was the whole team. Sheep do not like to provoke or displease. They are hypersensitive to reproach, and they cry easily.

Sheep are passive; they crave attention and approval and daydream about finding long-lasting love. They are complex people who can be timid and quiet one minute and determined and free-spoken the next.

Sheep prefer to hang out with strong-willed people to

complement their reticent nature. Most people will find Sheep to be fun partners, friends, colleagues, and family members. They are hard workers who like to play. Sheep function best when a balance is found between the creative and disorganized sides of their personality; but even with that balance, they suffer unnecessarily with anxiety when they are overly stressed.

 HER HEART

A prissy miss, the Ewe is a true princess. She is fanatical about her personal hygiene and her home. While it may be cluttered—strewn with notes to herself, articles of clothing, or her children's toys—it's sanitary. The kitchen, especially, is always neat—everything is washed well and in its proper place.

Men, beware, the lady Sheep is a flirt. Like a French coquette, she is beguiling and alluring without flaunting her sexuality. She is childlike, innocent, and wildly irresistible. Men want to take care of this seemingly helpless Ewe, but looks can be deceiving. She may appear powerless, but she can stand up for herself. Although it's true that she isn't a pushover, she does have a sensitive soul, so tread gently on her heart.

The lady Sheep is kind and compassionate. She's always available to help anyone who needs support or a comforting word. In a relationship, she makes an eager and devoted partner. In the office, she's always willing to stay late and lend a helping hand. Just call her Miss Congeniality.

The Ewe doesn't usually go into business for herself because she's shy by nature. However, when she does, her success is due to her compromising character for she is willing to accommodate, sometimes more than she should.

The Sheep likes to graze. Small meals and snacks keep her going throughout the day. Since she doesn't like to exercise, the inevitable result is an expanding waistline and a tendency toward poor health down the road. Therefore, it's important for the Sheep to find a sport that suits her inactive lifestyle, even if it's simply walking a mile or two a day. If a Ewe and a Ram marry, they will both tend toward portliness unless they work hard to keep off the weight.

The eyes of a Ewe are her best physical feature—deep pools of liquid lust that trap an unsuspecting mate. She makes a wonderful, loving mother. If her marriage should break apart, she will immediately look for another mate because she doesn't like to be alone. Although she is perfectly capable of living on her own, she feels out of sorts, antsy—as though something is missing. Her choices of men are not always the best. She'd rather settle than wait for Mr. Perfect to come along. The best lessons a female Sheep can learn are: she is stronger than she thinks she is, and it is perfectly okay to be alone.

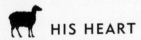 ## HIS HEART

The masculine Ram is in touch with his feminine side— and he's proud of it. He can appreciate nature and bask in its beauty without feeling as though he's a sissy. But don't be fooled by his willingness to give in. He's persistent and good at finding ways to make others bend to his will. For instance, if a lady rejects his marriage proposal, he will buy another engagement ring and propose again—including a dozen roses and a poem that gushes with sentiment. Who could turn that down? Spending money is one of the male Sheep's pleasures—if it helps him get the lady of his dreams, all the better.

Although he may have been skinny as a youngster, as he ages, he'll broaden out until his belly is hanging over his belt. Unless he gets his eating habits under control, he's a prime candidate for heart problems.

Sheep are not comfortable bossing others around and prefer jobs where they are part of a team, perhaps an accountant, stockbroker, writer, or doctor. That doesn't mean they can't be their own bosses—many are—they simply prefer not to have the whole burden on their shoulders. They are more like Oxen in this respect, although they are less plodding and more meandering, changing jobs as better opportunities come along.

Male Sheep are turned on by shows of appreciation. They want to be respected and adored. They make great dads and love spending time with their children at sporting events, both watching and participating. He'd rather be at home than at work, so it's important that they have a comfortable place to live. It doesn't have to be a castle, just homey.

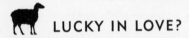

LUCKY IN LOVE?

The Ewe, with her long lashes that flutter whenever she wants something, is not shy about playing the field until she settles down for good. She is gentle in bed and not aggressive, and she's not adverse to trying new things. She expects her lover to be a gentleman at all times.

The Ram will wine and dine his honey until he gets what he wants from her, whether it's a one-night stand, a long-term affair, or marriage. He is the master of seduction and very inventive in bed. Unlike the female Sheep, he has a lusty appetite and is a capable lover when he's in the mood.

Jealousy does not suit the Sheep; nevertheless, it's part of the package. Neither the Ram nor the Ewe will tolerate their mates straying into someone else's bed—there will be hell to pay if they find out.

The most important aspect to making a relationship work with a Sheep is to be affectionate and understanding, since they thrive on love and loathe discord. They are smart, quirky, touchy-feely people who are romantic at heart.

FOR BETTER OR WORSE

Sheep and Tiger: The Tiger wants to protect the Sheep, and the Sheep will listen to the Tiger's many problems. They move in the same circle of friends and may even have the same profession. But the ties that bind are not as strong as they appear to outsiders. They need to be wary of confrontations that may cause a permanent rift. If this is you: Sort out problems as they arise—and stay calm while discussing sensitive matters to keep the love flowing without interruption.

Sheep and Rabbit: Shy and docile, these two make a loving couple. Each is appreciative of the other; neither wants to yell, fuss, or make a scene. Confrontations are not part of the picture. Both appreciate nature and the beauty of life. This touchy-feely pair have eyes only for each other and don't let small issues grow into big ones. If this is you: You two are a blissful pair, but try to be a little more decisive or you both may get frustrated and bored now and then.

Sheep and Sheep: Like minds, like hearts, like interests, the Ram and Ewe are a sympathetic and creative pair. The main drawback to this near-perfect union may be a lack of decision. This wishy-washy attitude can hurt them in business and in things they enjoy doing together. Being unable to decide where to go on vacation could ruin a perfectly fine time together. Otherwise, this is an A+ pair. If this is you: You two should brainstorm a list of things you like or want to do—when you're both being indecisive, you can avoid complications by randomly picking something off the list.

Sheep and Horse: These two personalities, although different in many ways, mesh beautifully. The Horse is straightforward and ambitious, which the Sheep admires.

The Sheep is talented and good-natured, which the Horse cherishes. The Horse is dominant, the Sheep compliant, which make an excellent match. If this is you: You're both golden in this comfortable union—enjoy!

Sheep and Dog: While these two may not have much in common, they both want harmony. The Sheep tends to wander. The Dog, on the other hand, works steadily toward a goal. The Sheep worries, and the Dog is prone to bouts of depression. If they can get past these glitches, they have a good chance of sticking together. If this is you: You both may need to make a concentrated effort to get along with your mate, but it will pay off in the long run.

Sheep and Pig: Talk about soul mates. The Pig always has a shoulder for the Sheep to cry on and will bolster the Sheep's sagging spirits whenever needed. The Pig and Sheep both enjoy the finer things life has to offer and will indulge themselves without worry or guilt. Excess is the downfall of this pair. They love each other deeply, but they may not be as healthy as they could be. If this is you: You'll need to join a gym, find a physical activity you both enjoy, or give up your cars if you two are going to stay healthy—no matter what, your relationship will be just fine.

Sheep and Rat: The Sheep is creative and sociable while the Rat is a workaholic who wants to operate alone. The Rat bottles up emotions, but the Sheep needs to talk through his or her problems. Eventually, this lack of communication will cause bad feelings on both sides. If this is you: You're in for some hard times unless you decide to be patient and communicate. The Rat needs to be more appreciative of the Sheep's talents, and the Sheep needs to be more supportive of the Rat's clever schemes.

Sheep and Ox: A stubborn Ox and a placid Sheep aren't the best mix of personalities. The Ox plods through life one step at a time, and the Sheep wanders off smelling the roses and forgets all about the task at hand. The Ox doesn't take kindly to this and badgers the Sheep, which causes the Sheep to chafe under the unreasonable restrictions. In order to keep the Sheep from wandering away, the Ox needs to give it a rest and be more accepting. If this is you: Be aware that the differences in your animal natures are a good thing, so stop trying to change your partner and life will be rosier.

Sheep and Dragon: The Dragon controls this union with unsubtle domination. The Sheep compromises, happy to be protected by the powerful Dragon. While this may seem like a mismatched pair, a sympathetic and uplifting Dragon can inspire the shy, creative Sheep to blossom creatively and ultimately benefit them both. The Dragon should take note that an overbearing nature does not sit well with the docile Sheep, and it would be better to tone it down. If this is you: You'll both get what you need out of this pair. Just remember to keep in mind the other's feelings and you should do just fine.

Sheep and Snake: The loving Sheep may be frustrated by the intellectual Snake, who doesn't want to indulge the Sheep's whims. This is too bad because they could benefit from each other's experience. The Snake could give the Sheep direction, and the Sheep could warm the Snake's cool nature. The Snake could also give the lackadaisical Sheep a kick in the pants to get things done. If this is you: You two have so much positive potential—if you can only learn to get along! Try seeking outside assistance because with the right help, you may find yourselves in a pleasurable, lifelong learning experience.

Sheep and Monkey: The slow-moving Sheep may be overwhelmed by the Monkey's high-spirited, money-making mentality. The Monkey is all business. The Sheep is more emotional. The Monkey always has a trick up his sleeve, which causes the Sheep to worry. The Monkey is clever, and the Sheep is creative. If this is you: You two have a shot if you're both committed to working hard at accepting your differences.

Sheep and Rooster: The Rooster is a disciplinarian and a critical manager. The Sheep does not take kindly to the Rooster's constant needling, and the Rooster finds the Sheep exasperating and much too wishy-washy. The Rooster wants to run the show and feels the Sheep should conform, but the Sheep wants no part of it and will not be put in a pen. If this is you: You two aren't a fun pair. If the Rooster refuses to cut the Sheep some slack, you'll always have problems.

WRITTEN IN THE STARS

Celebrity unions are fairly easy to analyze when we see them in terms of the Chinese zodiac. Since most people are familiar with the players, let's see why this handsome couple didn't last.

Georgia-born Julia Roberts was born on October 28, 1967, under the sign of the capricious Sheep. Her list of lovers is half a mile long. From actor Keifer Sutherland—to whom she was engaged—to Lyle Lovett, whom she married briefly, this world-famous Sheep is the queen of fickle hearts. Just look at this Pretty Woman's lustrous brown eyes, and you'll see why they are her most alluring feature.

One of her many suitors was television star Benjamin Bratt, who was born December 16, 1963, under the sign of the Rabbit. The Sheep and the Rabbit are blessed with good fortune and make a loving pair. Each appreciates the other, and neither is confrontational. Although Roberts and Bratt were together for three years and appeared destined for the altar, something went wrong.

Female Sheep can change their minds as quickly as the wind blows. Their fickle, spunky spirit leads them to believe something better is around the corner. They subscribe to the "grass is always greener" theory of life. Bratt wanted to settle down and start a family, something Rabbits are intent on doing. Sheep like to graze, and she wasn't ready to settle down until she met cameraman Daniel Moder on the set of *The Mexican*. They married in July 2002. How long it will last is anyone's guess.

The Wild, Witty Monkey

Years of the Monkey: 1908, 1920, 1932, 1944, 1956, 1968, 1980, 1992, and 2004

Famous Monkeys: Leonardo da Vinci, Julius Caesar, Elizabeth Taylor, Michael Douglas, Danny DeVito, Jennifer Aniston, and Tom Hanks

Season: Summer

Best qualities: Clever, amusing, inventive, business-minded, accomplished, vivacious, quick-witted, and enthusiastic

Worst qualities: Tricky, egotistical, verbose, unfaithful, unprincipled, and snobbish

THE WILD, WITTY MONKEY'S PERSONALITY

Monkeys are intelligent, quick-witted, and clever—just like their animal counterparts. Those lucky enough to come into the world on these special years are excellent at solving problems, have great linguistic flare, excel in business, and find success in whatever they do.

Monkeys are confident to a fault, and their inflated egos may get in the way of long-term relationships. They can become so impressed with their own self-importance that even their best friends tire of their snobbishness. That doesn't bother the resourceful Monkey, however. There are plenty of people who'd like to be their friend. Who wouldn't want to be razzled and dazzled with their witty sense of humor?

Monkeys, with their gift of gab and their ability to fascinate and charm, make great politicians, actors, and lawyers. They are fun to be around, but they can also be secretive and controlling—especially in matters of scheduling. In fact, they loathe boundaries of any sort. They scoff at speed limits on the highway, but their verbal talents save them from getting tickets every time.

To understand the Monkey, think of the children's book character Curious George and all the mischief he caused. That's the Monkey for you—inventive, mischievous, and insatiably curious. Monkeys are quick to come up with new inventions and creative ways of doing things. But then they may bore you to tears talking about how wonderful they are.

Because Monkeys are so resourceful and adept at

breezing through life and wiggling out of tight spots, they are judged harshly and criticized often. However, it takes more than a few words of discouragement to keep them down. And, in fact, it takes quite a bit of bad news to lead them into a fit of despair.

Like Rabbits, Monkeys prefer to avoid confrontation. But unlike Rabbits, whose feelings are easily hurt, Monkeys merely feel that arguments serve no purpose. Monkeys' logical, linear reasoning always makes them feel as though they are right. Period. It can be exasperating to argue with them. They can talk rings around anyone's reasoning and come out victorious in the end. Monkeys love to say: "I'm right. End of story!"

Marketing, sales, public relations, politics, communications, law, telemarketing, and entertainment are fields in which Monkeys excel. Their silver tongues can tie up a deal quicker than you can say "okay." They don't like taking no for an answer and will find ways to wear you down until you agree.

Clever and quick-witted, self-employed Monkeys can take a start-up company and make it grow into a successful business. Monkeys do have a small conscience. When it pricks them, they will contribute to a charity or pick up the tab. As long as they get the last word in edgewise, they are happy campers.

🐒 HER HEART

It's a woman's prerogative to change her mind, and that's especially true of the female Monkey. She's as changeable as the weather, bouncing up and down—a bundle of excitable emotions. This high-strung quality tends to keep her on the thin side—they may be wiry, but they are strong.

Although she's not drop-dead gorgeous, the female Monkey has no problem attracting men with her lively spirit. She's like a glass of bubbly champagne when she's in a good mood. Young at heart, she can find humor in almost any situation, and she is fun to be around. The lady Monkey's biggest problem is that she worries too much. It's silly really, for worry doesn't accomplish much; and the Monkey is smart enough to know this.

When the female Monkey throws a party, it's bound to be a success. She will find a theme and get everyone into the mood with her boundless enthusiasm. And she will be the picture of perfection for she is diligent about her hair and her looks.

She is curious by nature and wants to experience as much as she can. She will try numerous sports, take up the latest dance craze, go to lectures, attend self-help seminars, and stock up on all of the bookstore's bestselling titles. She may even go back to school or take adult education classes to keep her brain precision-tuned. There's not much you can put over on this savvy, sassy gal. She's one of a kind with a spunk that makes her quite unique.

Not everyone will find a female Monkey lovable—or even likable. Her overblown sense of self and "I can do it better" attitude can be a turn-off. Her need to be right makes her a perfect fact checker, copyeditor, number-cruncher, or data entry clerk.

Although she frets when people don't like her, she is unstoppable, whether anyone approves of her projects or not. She is independent and headstrong, and she will not be held back by her flaws or by the standards of others.

 ## HIS HEART

The male Monkey is extremely clever and tricky—he's adept at saying one thing and meaning another. Don't hold that against him, however, for the male Monkey is a charming guy with plenty of worthy attributes. He is generous and will lavish presents on those he likes. He's a good friend, because he's compassionate and caring. The male Monkey, with his quick wit and lively repartee, is also the life of the party.

The male Monkey enjoys the finer things that money can buy and he feels he's worth it. He's on the fast track to success, even if it means taking a few shortcuts here and there. As a skilled salesman, he can sell the Brooklyn Bridge twice to the same person and feel no remorse that he's just pulled a fast one. He likes the expression: "Try it, you'll like it."

He is independent and loves adventure—he's not thrilled by the daily grind of marriage or dead-end jobs. Give him freedom. His adrenaline rush comes from being a daredevil—bungee jumping, parasailing, drag racing, flying, and hunting. In life and romance, the male Monkey is only interested in the thrill of the chase.

The male Monkey is not quick to commit, but it's hard to be angry at him for long. If you are mad, he will pour out his heart and profess his love. Then he will buy his woman—or women—a meaningful trinket and hope that all is well again.

The male Monkey can find his way out of a paper bag—blindfolded. He cannot be trapped into anything— including unsavory business dealings or marriage. When cornered, he will do anything to break free again. So beware. Don't try to trap this wiseguy or you may find yourself high and dry—or worse, stranded at the altar.

 LUCKY IN LOVE?

For the female Monkey, appearance is everything. She likes to be seen in nice cars with well-groomed hunks. And he better have a nifty set of wheels.

She is not shy about taking the lead when it comes to pursuing men. Count on this feisty female to make the first move. She's a lusty lover and very inventive, but she likes to hop from bed to bed until she tires of the love games. In her early years, she likes the thrill of dating many men; but as she gets older, she decides to settle down.

The male Monkey is extremely attracted to women and he loves to have "arm candy" when he's out on the town.

He's the master seducer and delights in dreaming up new ways of getting his lady love into bed. The longer she resists, the more intrigued he becomes. The chase is a turn-on. The promise of excitement eggs him on until the conquest is complete.

Basically the male Monkey is a sweetheart unless a woman wants to nail him down with a marriage license.

Then he'll go swinging from the nearest vine without saying farewell. Remember ladies, this guy—while engaging and sweet, brainy and clever—should be taken with a grain of salt. If you're looking for marriage, you should look elsewhere.

While they may stay around for a while, neither the female or male Monkey is looking for a deep commitment or a long-term marriage. They want to have fun and explore the possibilities of love with as many partners as they can. They usually date several people at the same time, and they are so resourceful that it's easy for them to get away with it. Even if they're caught, they can squirm out of it somehow. Beware, you shouldn't always trust them; they are masters at deception—often they act innocent as Sheep even though they are guilty as sin.

FOR BETTER OR WORSE

Monkey and Rat: This is a winning combination since both want the best out of life and both are willing to work hard to get it. They get along so well because they're both clever, committed, cunning, enterprising, and resourceful—can we say enough good things about this passionate pair? If they let their positive traits dominate the union, they can have the best of all possible worlds. If this is you: You have everything going for you, so don't make mountains out of molehills when problems arise.

Monkey and Dragon: The clever, ambitious Monkey meshes well with the highly motivated, driven Dragon. In politics they are allies, but beware if one ego gets too big. These two dynamic personalities, who love to get involved in grand projects on a splendid scale, need to temper their enthusiasm and learn to share the responsibility. This is a passionate pair willing to experiment in bed and beyond. If this is you: You have the best of all things, so enjoy life to the max. If there is anything you feel is lacking, go get it!

Monkey and Horse: Two talented individuals, both working toward a common goal, make a formidable team. Talk about an abundance of energy! The Monkey and the Horse are an unbeatable duo. The Horse works hard and the Monkey provides a plethora of ideas. If this is you: This relationship is a win-win situation—if you can agree on the major issues and not sweat the little things.

Monkey and Rooster: The clever Monkey knows just how to handle the grumpy Rooster. The Monkey tunes out the Rooster's endless sarcasm and complaining and sees the big picture instead. The Rooster would do well to take a lesson from the Monkey and not be so petty. Although the Rooster wants to take the long, involved path and the Monkey looks for a shortcut, they can form a loving and passionate bond. If this is you: You two seem to have a natural balance of wills—enjoy!

Monkey and Dog: With mutual respect, these two can have a harmonious and profitable relationship, filled with much love and devotion. The affable Dog doesn't get involved in the Monkey's antics, but does appreciate the Monkey's clever nature. They both share friends and interests, which makes the bond even stronger. The Monkey finds the loyal Dog a marvelous helpmate. Together they can raise their kids with love and respect. If this is you: You two are a blissful pair—with the best of many worlds. You're never bored, but you enjoy the security of a stable union. You should relax and enjoy yourselves.

Monkey and Pig: The Monkey has clever ideas and the Pig has the cash to back them up. Together they can put an idea into action and enjoy the fruits of their labor. This suits them both since they like to make money. The Pig is less exuberant than the Monkey, but they have a common love of the good life, which helps them put petty differences to rest. If this is you: You're having fun and making money—what could be better?

Monkey and Ox: Take a clever, outgoing Monkey and put it with a stubborn, slow-moving Ox and there's bound to be trouble. The Monkey is simply too quick-witted for the methodical Ox. The only way to make this union work is if each accepts the other for what they are, without trying to change their partner's innate personality. If this is you: You'll need to learn a great deal about acceptance or leave—if you aren't willing to compromise, this relationship isn't going to work.

Monkey and Tiger: This is an excellent team, if only they would put their egos to rest. It's a game of one-upmanship between the Monkey and the Tiger, which doesn't make for a harmonious household. While the passion may be intense at times, bad feelings can erode that loving feeling. If this is you: You've nearly got what it takes to make a lasting relationship; but if you both won't share control, forget it. Nobody can be right all the time—share the load 50–50 and your chances of survival will increase tenfold.

Monkey and Rabbit: The trusting Rabbit will be hard-put to accept the clever Monkey's shenanigans. There is the possibility that they could get along, but the Monkey will have to work hard to convince the Rabbit that true love conquers all. At heart they are both optimists, which works in their favor; but the Monkey must take care not to run verbal rings around the Rabbit, which will surely be misconstrued and taken to heart. If this is you: You must be mindful of how you speak to each other—especially the Monkey. The Rabbit should learn to take the Monkey's chatter with a grain of salt.

Monkey and Snake: The Snake doesn't believe the Monkey for one minute. Everything that comes out of the Monkey's jabbering mouth is suspect to the Snake. Likewise, the Monkey finds the Snake's cold attitude unsettling and chafes when the Snake clams up completely. Instead of building a relationship based on their good points, they will spend their time pointing out each other's faults. If this is you: You're both better off alone—life's too short to feel so frustrated and misunderstood.

Monkey and Sheep: The shy, creative Sheep is no match for the lively, intelligent Monkey. This is not a marriage made in heaven. But there is hope if the Sheep is willing to let the Monkey manage the business end of their creative venture. Passion comes in fits and spurts, and the best advice for the Monkey is to take it down a notch. If this is you: Life is too short to race through it. Stop and smell the roses, and this relationship might work.

Monkey and Monkey: Take two like-minded individuals who love to explore new places and dabble in new and exciting ventures and you'd think this was a match made in heaven. It is—almost. Two Monkeys are on the go from morning to night. They talk rings around each other, but the problem is that they don't really hear each other. If this is you: You two need to slow down and communicate. If you do, all things are possible.

 ## WRITTEN IN THE STARS

Celebrity unions are fairly easy to analyze when we see them in terms of the Chinese zodiac. Since most people are familiar with the players, let's see how the Monkey fares in this roundup.

Legendary beauty Elizabeth Taylor was born in London, England, on February 27, 1932, under the sign of the Monkey.

If it's a woman's prerogative to change her mind, Ms. Taylor is a shining example. She's been married eight times, twice to actor Richard Burton. She has always been a social butterfly; and at age seventy, she is as busy as ever—campaigning for AIDS research, promoting her six perfume lines, and spreading good cheer around Tinseltown. Friends say she is as lively and vivacious as ever, despite numerous surgeries and illnesses.

We'd need another whole book to take a look at all the different combinations of signs that comprise Ms. Taylor's marriage list. But for the sake of curiosity, let's look at Welsh actor Richard Burton.

Richard Burton was born November 10, 1925, under the sign of the Ox. He and Taylor met in the early 1960s while filming the movie *Cleopatra*. He was married and so was she—to Eddie Fisher. The passion between these two international stars could not be denied; and they married in March 1964, after obtaining divorces from their respective spouses.

The marriage wasn't an easy match. Looking at the description of these two signs, it's easy to see why it wouldn't work. The Monkey is outgoing and clever, while the Ox is stubborn and slow-moving. To make it work, they needed total, unconditional acceptance of each other's personalities. But neither was going to change at that stage in his or her life, no matter how much they wanted to stay together.

The two reconciled and divorced again in 1976, showing that love and romantic passion aren't always enough to keep a relationship in good health.

Despite her numerous marriages and divorces, Taylor has no problem attracting men with her lively spirit. Young at heart, Elizabeth Taylor still dazzles; and she says she has no intention of repeating her past mistakes. "I am not going to marry anybody who is on the face of this Earth or any other planet, ever, ever again!" claims the lavender-eyed beauty. Is she serious or is she just Monkeying around?

The Picky Rooster

Years of the Rooster: 1909, 1921, 1933, 1945, 1957, 1969, 1981, 1993, and 2005

Famous Roosters: Katharine Hepburn, Joan Collins, Melanie Griffith, Dolly Parton, John Glenn, Heather Graham, and Elton John

Season: Autumn

Best qualities: Candid, energetic, brave, clever, generous, spirited, stylish, adventurous, and confident

Worst qualities: Showy, shortsighted, pretentious, cheap, and nervy

THE PICKY ROOSTER'S PERSONALITY

The Rooster is the cock of the walk—isn't that a surprise? The Chinese consider the Rooster to be the most erratic of all the signs and for good reason. The Rooster can be clever, brave, self-assured, and confident and at the same time introspective, conservative, pretentious, and a royal pain in the rear.

There are Roosters who are fast-talking, quick-thinking, high-powered balls of energy. And there are other Roosters who are quiet, pensive, introverted observers of life. Often these are two sides of the same person. One thing is for sure—Roosters don't miss much.

Neat and organized, Roosters have an eye for detail. They speak their minds, too often without considering other's feelings. Their frankness can be hurtful, so don't ask for an honest opinion unless you want the brutal truth. Forget about discretion or finesse, for these social gadabouts have virtually no tact. But put them in the limelight and you've got a witty, entertaining ham. Roosters are talented as actors, art gallery directors, museum curators, writers, comics, salespeople, scientists, and photographers; but they make very poor diplomats because they lack tact.

Roosters are opinionated to a fault. They have to be right, which wears down their friends and loved ones. Take them with a grain of salt. Sometimes it's easier to agree than to ruffle their feathers—if not, there will be a scene. Roosters' egotistical behaviors are sometimes masks for their deep insecurities—a fact they don't want anyone to ever find out about.

Roosters are penny pinchers. They are excellent with money and they know how to squirrel it away. Living on a budget is second nature to them—they also budget time and energy. Roosters find happiness in occupations that revolve around money, such as accounting, auditing, bookkeeping, stock brokering, or working in a bank, or for the Internal Revenue Service. Roosters keep all accounts current because they detest paying late fees.

Roosters exhibit many fine qualities, but sometimes this fact is overshadowed by their endless needling and fault-finding. It's simply their nature to disagree about the smallest details, so it's important not to take it personally. Unfortunately, this bad habit of harping about every little thing even carries into the bedroom as well—being romantically involved with Roosters can be tough.

If the Rooster could learn that a little sweet talking goes a long way in the romance department, life would be a lot sweeter. Instead, the Rooster lavishes gifts as a way of apologizing for rude behavior. Saying "I'm sorry" would be better, but don't hold your breath. Getting a Rooster to admit making a mistake isn't going to happen. As you would expect, the Rooster's favorite expression is: "Why did you do it *that* way?"

It would help Roosters relax if they understood that perfection is only a state of mind, not a tangible reality. Even if they are critical, fussy task masters who worry over trifles and reach for impossible dreams, the fact remains that they have good hearts and make loyal mates.

🐓 HER HEART

The Hen is not shy about crowing. She takes great pride in her appearance. Her hair is stylishly coifed, her nails are manicured, and her clothes are pressed and appropriate for any occasion. Her eyes are clear and focused—she sees all.

She's not a shrinking violet—she meets the world head on and challenges anyone who gets in her way. Her rigid outlook on life irritates some people. But the Hen isn't afraid of confrontation. She speaks her mind freely and without constraint. Yet she has great compassion for those more timid than she. Although she appears fearsome, she can be a good friend and a loyal helpmate.

The Hen's favorite expression is: "I have a better way to do that." Flexibility is not her strong point. She's a no-nonsense, take-charge gal who believes she's always right. Forget about disagreeing with her. She won't take no for an answer. On the other hand, if you want a project finished in perfect order and on time—or ahead of schedule—give it to the lady Rooster. Her intense energy allows her to juggle many balls in the air without dropping a single one.

She is organized and efficient and sticks to a perfect, set routine. The lady Rooster wakes up, eats, goes to sleep, and does just about everything else at the same time every day. When she's thrown off her feet, so to speak, she gets irritated and begins pecking.

With food in her belly and eight hours of beauty rest, this perfectionist is the most spirited of all of the signs. She is a born leader, a diligent worker, and an asset to any organization. There are virtually no jobs where the lady Rooster will not excel. Any employer would do well to hire this feisty female, even if she does have an "attitude." In spite of this small shortcoming, she is loyal, skilled, and eminently capable of completing any task.

You can count on the fact that she'll get to know everyone else's intimate secrets, but don't expect her to spill the beans about her own private life. This clever lady is looking for your weaknesses. When the time comes, she will take deadly aim and let loose with a zinger that will make you wonder why you ever trusted her with your most personal news.

Be careful not to cross the lady Rooster; if you do, she'll peck and peck at you until she's satisfied you have been sufficiently punished. And don't think you have any chance of getting off the hook by flattering her; although she loves to be complimented, her brusque nature will not tolerate nonsense.

HIS HEART

Generally speaking, male Roosters are hunky, good-looking guys—and they know it. They strut about with a magnetism that is exciting and daunting. Their energy is awesome, but much of it stems from their naturally high-strung nature.

The male Rooster is constantly in motion, and he'll blurt out whatever is on his mind without thinking about the consequences. Never ask him a question unless you are prepared to hear an honest answer. You might not like what you hear.

The male Rooster's favorite expression is: "Tell me what's on your mind." He wants to know all, but don't expect him to tell you anything. It's not his character. His mind is a data bank for all this information; and he can use it to help or hinder, so beware of crossing him—he can be treacherous. You'll never get him to admit he's wrong.

Brash and outspoken, male Roosters often settle on careers where they can grandstand, such as: show business, law, politics, or the arts. Taking on causes and becoming involved in local government allows male Roosters to talk the talk and walk the walk.

The male Rooster makes a loyal family man. He is devoted to friends and loved ones. Although he tries to be a responsible dad, he doesn't always succeed because he finds it hard to put anyone before himself. He is a harsh disciplinarian and rigid in his thinking, but he knows how to have fun—when he lets his guard down and hangs loose.

LUCKY IN LOVE?

The lady Rooster is very difficult to live with. Her tongue is razor-sharp and stings like a scorpion when you least expect it. As the ruler of the roost, she likes to find weaker men and boss them around. Naturally, she loses respect for them in no time and moves on to her next conquest. Although she says she wants to fall madly and passionately in love, she holds back to avoid making a fool of herself. After all, what could be worse than looking irrational? The Hen does not take rejection well—or lightly—but it's inevitable since it's her nature to harp on her partner until he picks up and leaves. For the man who can tame his feisty female, the reward is a passionate, sexy lover with a good heart and a sweet disposition.

Sex is important for the male Rooster. He is highly charged and erotic and imagines himself a great lover, which he may be. Certainly he tries hard because pleasing a woman is very important to his macho image. He likes nothing better than to have his lady brag to her friends about what a stud he is in bed. While he finds it hard to express his feelings and will rarely say "I love you," he is capable of deep caring and genuine love.

🐓 FOR BETTER OR WORSE

Rooster and Ox: The steadfast Ox can handle the flamboyant Rooster without any problems. The Ox is not bothered by the Rooster's criticism or quest for perfection. The Ox's calm demeanor can soothe the hyperactive Rooster. They are both determined to reach their goals and are thoughtful planners. Home life is important to them both. If this is you: You two can always be sure of at least two things: you're home will always run like clockwork, and you'll never need to search for another love. Your personalities are a great match—your relationship is in the bag.

Rooster and Tiger: Neither of these signs shies away from controversy, which works to their favor. The Tiger, who may be more diplomatic and charming than the hot-tempered Rooster, admires the Rooster's enthusiasm and lust for living. The Rooster enjoys being out in social situations with the suave, smooth-talking Tiger. Although opposites in many ways, these two are filled with a zest for living and well suited for each other. If this is you: You'll both be happy in this union—things will never be boring, but chaos isn't likely either.

Rooster and Dragon: The Dragon's passion and the Rooster's vivacity make this a winning pair. Both have huge egos; and if they don't let this issue drive a wedge between them, they can find long-lasting peace together. The Rooster's faultfinding rolls off the Dragon's back, and the Rooster appreciates the Dragon's boldness. Together they are a formidable team in any undertaking. If this is you: You're sure to do just fine so long as you keep those egos in check—remember, humbleness is a very important trait. Make sure you express your appreciation for the other's good qualities instead of always talking about your own.

Rooster and Snake: The clever Snake is a perfect match for the egotistical Rooster. The Snake and Rooster are both ambitious, artful, and frugal with their money. The Rooster's ranting can't rattle the cool, calm, and collected Serpent. They can live an insulated life, away from the social scene and be very happy with their joint ventures and their family life. If this is you: You two run a tight ship—don't forget to go out every once in a while and enjoy what the spontaneity of reality has to offer.

Rooster and Monkey: The clever Monkey knows just how to handle the cantankerous Rooster. The Monkey tunes out the Rooster's sarcasm and complaining and doesn't sweat the small stuff. Monkeys focus on the big picture, looking for shortcuts; while the Rooster wants to take the long winding road to get wherever they are going. Despite these obvious differences, they can form a loving and passionate bond. If this is you: You need to remember that a give-and-take attitude works best. Don't forget that compromise goes a long way toward keeping the peace.

Rooster and Pig: The ambitious Pig appreciates the arrogant Rooster and is not bothered by the Rooster's critical nature. The thick-skinned Pig lets the windbag carp all day long and pays no mind. The Pig is generous by nature and the Rooster is not; but despite this small difference, their personalities mesh surprisingly well as long as they respect each other's opinions. If this is you: You may argue more than many couples, but making up keeps the love strong between you. Always remember to kiss goodnight and that nobody has to be right all the time.

Rooster and Rat: Talk about contention. With these two, it's a never-ending contest of wills. Picky and particular, the hotheaded Rooster and the petty, power-hungry Rat will play the one-upmanship game until they are worn out. Although they both have excellent qualities, when they are together, the worst in both take over. If this is you: You two need to stay far away from each other—life is too short to be so miserable.

Rooster and Rabbit: These opposites don't attract at all. Their outlook and approach to life is not compatible and they have little in common. Their relationship will be fraught with friction, and the Rabbit will not be able to stand the Rooster's verbal barrage of insults. Since the Rabbit doesn't like strife, this is a lose-lose situation from the start unless the Rooster is mindful of the Rabbit's sensitive feelings. If this is you: Your relationship isn't doomed to certain failure, but it's going to be very difficult. You'll both need to compromise a lot or throw in the towel.

Rooster and Horse: The Horse likes to be in control, which will freak the Rooster out. The Rooster will find fault with the Horse, which will not sit well on the Horse's independent shoulders. Being reprimanded is not the Horse's cup of tea. Although they are both hard working, bright individuals, their temperaments are not well suited for a long-term commitment unless each stays positively focused. If this is you: You two need a lot of patience and some outside help to work out this messy pairing.

Rooster and Sheep: The creative Sheep is far too sensitive for the critical Rooster. And the uptight Rooster finds the laid-back Sheep too easygoing and unenthusiastic. The Sheep is not comfortable with the Rooster's rules and inflexibility. If this is you: Unless the Rooster employs more give-and-take in the relationship, the Sheep will find greener pastures to graze in elsewhere.

Rooster and Rooster: This bickering pair will inevitably peck themselves into a parting of the ways. How can two excitable personalities with barbed tongues—each of whom has to be right and running the show—find a common ground upon which they can build a relationship? Their verbal sparring will either drive a wedge between them or make them into a bitter old couple. If this is you: You both need to objectively evaluate the situation and weigh the pros and cons—if you decide to stay together, seek outside help.

Rooster and Dog: There is a possibility these two can get along, but it will take some work. The Dog is a loyal companion who takes the Rooster's harping with dignified patience, although the Dog doesn't see why the Rooster must make mountains out of molehills. If the Rooster is impressed with the Dog's steadfast nature, he or she may try to be less overbearing and more accepting. If this is you: Be prepared to put in a lot of work if you want to make a long-term relationship blossom.

🐓 WRITTEN IN THE STARS

Celebrity unions are fairly easy to analyze when we see them in terms of the Chinese zodiac. Since most people are familiar with the players, let's see if this dynamic couple can survive the difference in their ages and their signs.

Gorgeous Catherine Zeta-Jones was born in Swansea, Wales on September 25, 1969, under the sign of the Rooster. She began her career in a stage production of *Annie*. Her breakthrough role in *The Mask of Zorro* (1998) showcased her proud and defiant Rooster qualities. Michael Douglas was born under the sign of the Monkey on September 25, 1944—that's exactly twenty-five years (to the day) before Catherine. When Michael Douglas saw her, he was instantly smitten and decided right then and there to pursue her despite their age difference. Clever Douglas knew just how to handle the self-assured raven-haired Rooster. Monkeys don't sweat the small stuff. Instead they see the big picture—even if the Rooster tends to pick at details.

"I've never dated anybody the same age as me," Zeta-Jones told *People* magazine in the October 11, 1999, issue. "I think it's because I love the knowledge older men have."

The chemistry between these two superstars is magical. Their first child, Dylan Michael Douglas, was born in 2000, a few months before they married.

Because the picky Rooster and the clever Monkey are compatible signs according to the Chinese zodiac, they should have a long and happy union as long as the Monkey doesn't get bent out of shape when the Rooster begins fussing.

The Diligent Dog

Years of the Dog: 1910, 1922, 1934, 1946, 1958, 1970, 1982, 1994, and 2006

Famous Dogs: Winston Churchill, Mother Teresa, Sophia Loren, Elvis Presley, Sally Field, Cher, Jennifer Lopez, Matt Damon, and Madonna

Season: Autumn

Best qualities: Generous, fearless, loyal, faithful, altruistic, respectful, bright, devoted, and rational

Worst qualities: Cautious, introverted, hypercritical, defensive, pessimistic, obstinate, unsociable, and preachy

THE DILIGENT DOG'S PERSONALITY

The personality traits of Dogs give new meaning to the adage "You can't teach an old dog new tricks." On the whole, male and female Dogs are loving, kind, honest, hard working, humorous, and loyal. They are also set in their ways.

Dogs are the most likable sign in the Chinese zodiac. They are easy to get along with, and they aren't pretentious or demanding. They will meet you halfway—or even travel the whole distance, if need be. They are very responsible and always pull their own weight—and they'd never ask others to do something they wouldn't do themselves.

If you have only one friend, make sure it's somebody born under this sign. Dogs stick like glue, through thick and thin, to those they love. Many relationships last far longer than expected because of the Dog's incredible devotion. With a shoulder always available for friends to cry on and an ear for listening to problems, they are sympathetic, sensitive, compassionate, and tender. Their optimistic attitude makes their favorite expression: "This, too, shall pass. Things will get better someday."

Dogs make worthy allies. They root for the underdog, naturally, and are especially avid supporters of just causes. They are people you can count on to be there and to carry through to the end. Dogs dislike hypocrisy and will not tolerate lying, cheating, or stealing. Their morals are high and their tolerance for deceitfulness is low.

People under this sign are born to be public defenders,

fundraisers, crusaders, religious leaders, psychologists, and caregivers. Instinctively, Dogs intuit who can be trusted and who should not. They can sniff out the good and the bad with unerring accuracy. Their assessments of human nature are invariably correct.

Dogs don't socialize much. They'd rather be home having a quiet evening than partying with friends until the wee hours of the morning. Perhaps the Dog works too hard, takes life too seriously, and worries too much. If they could learn to temper this solitary tendency, perhaps they would have more fun.

Beware of crossing Dogs—they can inflict a vicious bite. They never mince words, so you always know exactly what's wrong. Yet a Dog's bright and chipper attitude will usually mask this churlish side.

Although trustworthy, Dogs may seem standoffish. It will take a while before they warm up to you, but don't be discouraged—once they do, they are loyal and dependable friends and lovers.

Dogs thrive on love. They lap up tenderness and affection and positively glow when someone does something nice for them. On the flip side, they are pessimistic, and, therefore, usually suspicious of favors.

Dogs are devastated by rejection. It takes a long time for their hearts to heal and before they are able to love again. Dogs who are hurt early in life are exceptionally fearful of trying new things. It is very likely that they will decide to live alone rather than risk being maltreated again. Taking a chance on love is a huge step, and many Dogs simply are not willing to make themselves so vulnerable.

Dogs aren't too troubled by money. They are often born into it; and if they need more, they don't mind working harder. When in love, they are generous to a fault, but they can also be horribly frugal.

🐕 HER HEART

The female Dog appears glamorous, yet understated in her simple, elegant clothing. She's chic, not ostentatious. She wears subtle makeup and a hairstyle that shows off her face. The lady Dog makes people feel comfortable when they are in her presence. Even celebrities born under this sign are approachable and not snobbish.

Although the female Dog appears warm and friendly, you'll have to work hard to get into her heart—whether romantically or as a friend. The lady Dog is wary of strangers and doesn't open up easily. But once you are accepted into her inner sanctum, she will go to the ends of the earth for you.

People listen when female Dogs speak. Expect to find them as champions of the less fortunate, on charity committees, and supporting causes like the environment and women's issues. Once they have chosen purposes, they will donate time, money, and enormous amounts of energy to their crusades. Their stamina is remarkable, and they're cool under pressure. Don't expect lady Dogs to buckle under anyone's demands. On the whole, female Dogs are cooperative and easygoing; but when crossed, they are snappy and curt and will cut people off in mid-sentence and walk away.

Although she always appears busy, the female Dog knows how to stop and smell the roses. She loves being outdoors. She's in heaven when she's in the country—urban life is too stressful and pretentious for her.

Sitting around doing nothing may be what real dogs do, but not women born under the sign of the Dog. The female Dog is constantly on the move, doing, creating, fixing—she is a dynamo of energy. Her "busy as a bee" spirit helps to keep any mood swings from turning into full-blown depression. But she is prone to depression—especially when she takes the criticisms of others to heart. The lady Dog shies away from people who find fault with her style of living or her basic personality flaws. Although she is surrounded by love, the lady Dog tends to be sad. You can read it in her eyes. She is protective of herself because of her vulnerabilities. The lady Dog is shy at heart and lacks self-esteem, so she is afraid of being betrayed or getting hurt. When she is involved in romantic entanglements, she expects too much and is often disappointed.

She is an excellent, caring mother; and her top-notch organizational skills keep the household from running wild. She takes the weight of the world on her shoulders and somehow manages to thrive and give to others. The lady Dog is an altruistic, faithful, and modest person who gives far more of herself than she probably should.

HIS HEART

Although the well-meaning male Dog is not a high-spirited leader like the Horse or Dragon, he will surround himself with take-charge people and be carried along by their exuberance. On his own, he is an admirable planner and organizer; and others listen when he speaks.

Male Dogs can take plenty of stress and still remain calm, which makes them excellent therapists, clergymen, teachers, doctors, farmers, laborers, and social workers.

At heart, the male Dog is a skeptic and more than a little cynical about politics and life in general. He's not very spontaneous—he proceeds cautiously. Just watch him get into a pool or the ocean—one toe at a time, taking forever until his whole body is submerged. It would drive a Dragon crazy!

Unlike the cocky Rooster, there is nothing egotistical about the male Dog. He stands slightly stooped and walks awkwardly. Needless to say, his endearing charm makes him irresistible to some women. He's a bit of a goof, but his eyes are warm and loving—they can draw an unsuspecting heart right into his soul.

The parsimonious male Dog doesn't lavish frivolous gifts. Instead, he splurges on practical things that his lady can use for years to come. The male Dog only parts with his hard-earned dollars for top-of-the-line items that won't fall apart in five minutes.

Male Dogs admire and fear women at the same time. They want a loving relationship; and yet they are so afraid of rejection, that many remain bachelors and never marry—or marry for only a short time. They can be hard to live with because they are so critical, and they know this. They are set in their ways and don't compromise easily. Having dated a few women, he knows that love is a give-and-take; and he's reluctant to give too much of himself, preferring to keep his emotions bottled inside. Often, male Dogs forego the joys of marriage and family and opt for solitary lives where they can have their own way at all times.

For those male Dogs who have made the commitment to a long-term relationship, it is usually a good decision. They are pleasantly surprised and content to come home every night to a loving spouse. The lucky lady the male Dog settles down with will be able to count on him through thick and thin.

LUCKY IN LOVE?

The female Dog, with her gentle, unaffected nature, appeals to men who want a wholesome mate. She is modest, a bit on the prudish side, and needs to be coaxed into dating and into bed. Despite her outspoken nature, the lady Dog will not ask a man out first. Many female Dogs never marry, and those that do often get divorced.

Although shy and a bit reserved, the lady Dog is an excellent choice for a lifetime partner. However, it will be a challenge to make her fall in love with you. Her instincts say "beware," so you will need patience and perseverance to win her over. Instead of giving her expensive presents, show her that you can be trusted. That's more important than gifts.

When it comes to romance, the female Dog is awkward and reserved. She appears as green as an unripe banana, but she will mellow if she can bask in the presence of a man who truly cares for her—heart and soul.

The male Dog doesn't fall in love at first sight—he takes his time. He likes to get to know his lady as a friend first, before they become lovers, to see if they are compatible and if she can be trusted. You can't rush a Dog—it may take numerous dates before he wants to take a woman to bed. In the meantime, you may be wondering, "What's wrong? Doesn't he like me?" Don't worry, nothing is wrong, he's just trying to protect his heart. His caution is understandable; after all, he takes rejection very hard. So just be patient and have faith that he'll give himself totally once you've earned his trust.

FOR BETTER OR WORSE

Dog and Rat: Mutual respect makes this pair a good fit. The clever, ambitious Rat manages the household affairs, leaving the Dog to pursue worthy causes. There is little struggle for dominance because both are equal partners; and conflicts, while few and far between, are settled quickly and then forgotten. If this is you: You should consider yourselves blessed to have found each other—not everyone is so lucky.

Dog and Tiger: The extroverted and energized Tiger is a perfect complement to the shy but hard-working Dog. Together, they are caught up in the excitement of living and helping others less fortunate than they are. It's common for couples born under these signs to open their arms wide and become foster or adoptive parents to many children. If this is you: You two will always have a lot of cheer, a lot of laughs, and a lot of love—enjoy!

Dog and Rabbit: Trust is the glue that keeps these two signs together for the long haul. They speak the same language of mutual respect and both want the union to last, which means they will do what it takes to make it work. The Rabbit wants a peaceful, loving relationship; so does the Dog. If this is you: You are the envy of all your friends, and you should have a wonderful and happy union.

Dog and Horse: The high-spirited Horse works well with the diligent Dog. The Horse is aggressive, which helps the bashful Dog overcome that hang-up. Neither holds a grudge for long and neither is a nit-picker. Together they fight injustice and they get along famously. If this is you: When problems arise or you disagree, sit down and talk things out. Then kiss and make up and let bygones be bygones.

Dog and Sheep: While these two may not have much in common, they both want harmony. Of course, that's not enough to make for smooth sailing. The Sheep tends to wander; while the Dog, on the other hand, works steadily toward a goal. The Sheep worries when the Dog becomes sullen and silent. If they can get past these glitches, they have a good chance of sticking together. If this is you: The most important aspect of keeping this union running smoothly is communication. When the Dog shuts down, the Sheep will need a sense of humor to keep the dialogue going. Lighten up!

Dog and Dog: Take two kindhearted, sensitive people who love nature and supporting just causes and you have an unbeatable team. Two Dogs will admire each other; but because they are both shy and reserved, it may take them a while to get together. Given time and trust, they can have a marriage that endures through the years, even if there is occasional snarling and snapping. If this is you: You two have so much in common that you understand each other inside and out; and, don't worry, you'll never get bored because you'll always find new activities/causes to involve yourselves in.

Dog and Ox: The friendly, reserved Dog chafes under the strict Ox and may find the Ox's stubborn, unforgiving nature too difficult to deal with. They have mutual understanding when they are in sync working toward a common goal or raising a family, even if the Dog wants to rush along and the Ox wants to move at a slower pace. With a give-and-take attitude, they can succeed in making it work. If this is you: This relationship is a borderline case of two signs that can get along, but it will take flexibility on both parts to work.

Dog and Dragon: The Dog and the Dragon are direct opposites in the zodiac—together they make a poor match. The Dragon is showy and shallow, while the Dog is deep and shy. They have contrary outlooks on life, and this makes it difficult for them to understand one another. Like two pieces of flint rubbing against one another, sparks will fly. If this is you: Romance may be passionate at first, but you'll need plenty of courage and counseling if you want to stay together for the long haul.

Dog and Snake: The Dog may find it difficult to completely trust the cool, introspective Snake. The Dog admires the Snake's ambition, and the Snake likes the Dog's energy. Both are hard workers and compatible to a certain extent. With diligence, these two can work out their differences. If this is you: You must keep the lines of communication open. The Dog tends to sulk and the Snake slithers off to brood. Unless you talk things over, trouble will soon follow.

Dog and Monkey: The high-powered Monkey can be overwhelming, and the Dog's shy, retiring attitude can get on the Monkey's nerves. But as long as they understand this is simply their inborn nature and they can find a common ground from which to operate, they can make an industrious couple. The good news is that the Monkey knows not to tease the Dog, and the Dog enjoys the Monkey's sense of humor. If this is you: You two will do just fine if you learn to give each other a little space and try not to push each other too hard.

Dog and Rooster: The Dog's mood swings drive the Rooster crazy, while the Rooster's daredevil antics make the Dog fret. The patient Dog is put to the test by the Rooster's critical appraisal. The Rooster wants to change the bashful Dog, and the retiring Dog wants the Rooster to lighten up. If this is you: You're both going to be unhappy in this union. Even if you smooth over the surface problems, your incompatibility runs too deep to completely be repaired.

Dog and Pig: The conservative, frugal Dog will be appalled by the Pig's overindulgent lifestyle and will want the Pig to live less lavishly. The Pig does not want to change, and that's the crux of this couple's problem. In addition, the lusty Pig won't appreciate the Dog's prudish attitude when it comes to sex, which may lead to serious problems with intimacy. If this is you: There are many others that will make better partners. This couple will have to work very hard.

🐕 WRITTEN IN THE STARS

Celebrity unions are fairly easy to analyze when we see them in terms of the Chinese zodiac. Since most people are familiar with the players, let's see if this handsome couple has what it takes to keep the sparks flying.

To see how two Dogs get along, take a look at Susan Sarandon, born Susan Abigail Tomalin on October 4, 1946, in Jackson Heights, N.Y., and her longtime partner, Tim Robbins, born on October 16, 1958.

Sarandon began her career as a model, married actor Chris Sarandon, and made her film debut in 1970 in the movie *Joe*. She acted on daytime soap operas, then starred in a string of hits, including *The Rocky Horror Picture Show*, 1975; *Pretty Baby*, 1978; *Atlantic City* with Burt Lancaster, 1980; and *The Witches of Eastwick* in 1987 with Cher and Michelle Pfeiffer. She and Chris divorced after only a few years of marriage.

Susan and Tim met in 1988, during the filming of the baseball comedy *Bull Durham*. Although she was romanced by Kevin Costner on screen, her heart was captured by Tim Robbins, almost exactly twelve years her junior. Despite their age difference, these two Dog actors have been together ever since—their chemistry was tangible on screen.

True to the nature of the Dog, Sarandon and Robbins are kindhearted, sensitive people who love nature and fighting for the underdog. They are both well known for their political activism, and they are two of Hollywood's most outspoken celebrities. They are constantly crusading for one cause or another, while maintaining their respective careers and raising a family.

Sarandon and Robbins have two sons together, Jack Henry, born in May 1989, and Miles Guthrie, born in 1992. Susan also has a daughter, Eva Amurri, from a former relationship.

These two Dogs admire each other both on and off the screen. Susan basks in Robbins's presence; he glows in hers. Also conforming to the description above of a longer than usual courtship, this pair of entertainers has never married, even though they are committed to one another.

The Sensuous Pig

Years of the Pig: 1911, 1923, 1935, 1947, 1959, 1971, 1983, 1995, and 2007

Famous Pigs: Alfred Hitchcock, Lucille Ball, Julie Andrews, Steven Spielberg, Ernest Hemingway, John D. Rockefeller, and Hillary Rodham Clinton

Season: Autumn

Best qualities: Helpful, good-natured, kind, sensual, cultivated, decisive, peace-loving, sympathetic, and sincere

Worst qualities: Insecure, cynical, malicious, hedonistic, headstrong, rigid, naïve, and weak

THE SENSUOUS PIG'S PERSONALITY

The association of Pigs with banks is not an accident. Pigs are industrious workers, but their ultimate goal is to enjoy the fruits of their labor. They want to live in opulent surroundings, and the only way to do that is to put money aside, not only for a rainy day, but for retirement as well. In addition, as they age, they tend to become rotund—just like those bulging piggy banks.

Pigs are honest, simple folks who apply themselves to a given task and perform their duties with cheerful gallantry. While they may appear unpolished, underneath their rough exterior beat hearts of gold. Pigs want to live in harmony with others and, like the Sheep and Rabbit, do not like confrontations and shy away from violence. Instead of jumping into a chaotic situation, the Pigs dial 911.

You can count on the Pig to accept any invitation for a social gathering. With a drink in one hand and a canapé in the other, the Pig is a social schmoozer famed for introducing people who will get along, either in business or romance. The Pig is a good listener and will stay long enough to hear all of your troubles.

While they are rocks of stability and make terrific friends and excellent partners for business, romance, or politics, Pigs are gullible and make easy targets for scam artists. They believe that everyone is honest and filled with goodwill, thus they are vulnerable to swindlers and solicitations for bogus charities. Fortunately, their pals watch out for their best interests. Whether or not you've helped a Pig, they are always willing to raise money for a charitable cause or loan you money.

Pigs' boundless hearts are filled with commiseration for any friend or acquaintance who's in trouble. They will give you the shirt off their backs. While it may be true that they are pushovers, they are also some of the nicest people on Earth. In fact, their favorite expression is: "What's yours is mine."

Although it may appear that the kindhearted, well-mannered Pig is too good to be true, there is another side to the Pig that is less obvious: the Pig enjoys guilty pleasures. Basically, the Pig is a hedonist and wants as much gratification as possible. This indulgence can manifest itself in many ways, such as alcohol, rich food, drugs, chocolate, and the pursuit of sensuality. This self-indulgent side is offset by the Pig's generous nature when it comes to others. The Pig will always take time to provide comfort, give a smile, a hug, or a wad of cash, if that's what is needed to put things right again. The Pig has an ample sense of humor and remembers dozens of good jokes.

The charming Pig wants to be everyone's best friend. But the gracious Pig will not tolerate back-stabbing, bad-mouthing malcontents. There is no room for conflict in the Pig's peaceful world. Rather than get into an argument, the Pig will change the subject or walk away—that will be the end of the relationship. Perhaps it's to the Pig's detriment that he'd rather not deal directly with thorny issues. But nothing will change that. It's the Pig's nature. Despite any flaws, the Pig is still an excellent, beneficial partner to have.

 HER HEART

The lady Pig is a warm-hearted, compassionate woman, filled with good vibes and a rock-steady nature. She makes a wonderful mom and a marvelous helpmate who will spoil her piglets rotten. She will even fetch her hubby his slippers or a beer to keep him happy. She's an eager lover, so men swoon over her.

One ploy of the lady Pig is to appear helpless when, of course, she's not. She knows how to get exactly what she wants, and she wants a lot. But if fame and fortune don't smile upon her, that's okay, too. The female Pig is an adaptable creature who can be happy under almost any conditions—as long as she's doing something productive.

Lady Pigs make fine homemakers, nurses, caretakers, teachers, creative artists, businesswomen, and politicians. They can act, sing, dance, and bake apple pies—all at the same time, as long as nobody rushes them along. They are content to be at home with their families, their projects, and their own space. Then again, they can also climb the corporate ladder and break the glass ceiling if they so desire. Female Pigs can do anything they set their minds to.

The lady Pig doesn't like to be criticized. In fact, she has no problem lashing out if she is provoked. When mean-spirited people take advantage of her, she feels hurt and vulnerable. At that low point, the female Pig is a sitting duck for bullies, con men, or people less virtuous than she is. Take cover if you have wronged a lady Pig—she will retaliate. Don't expect her to forgive and forget; the lady Pig can hold a grudge until hell freezes over.

Female Pigs love to pass their time daydreaming. They are romantic by nature, and they adore love stories and romantic comedies.

The lady Pig wants a husband who is in a money-making profession so she can live comfortably. Of course, she could go out and earn her own money. If she isn't taking care of a house of piglets, that's exactly what she will do. With a brood at home, she is bound to be involved in the P.T.A. and other school organizations and functions. She's a soccer mom, attending sporting events no matter how bad the weather; chairing fundraising committees; or lending a helping hand where needed. Her children are her biggest priority, and she is extraordinarily patient with them.

As for exercising, the lady Pig isn't interested in improving her physique. She would rather do anything but work out or diet; and she tends to gain weight, so it's important that she takes care of her health. The female Pig would do well to find a lifestyle that will keep her in shape. Regardless of her size or shape, she is a reliable friend, a trusted mate, and a truly nice person.

HIS HEART

The male Pig is a stickler for propriety. He doesn't like deceptive people. He is honest as the day is long—even gullible to some extent.

The male Pig lives in the now—concerned with today, not yesterday or tomorrow. He has a pragmatic attitude and rolls with the punches when misfortune hits. His favorite expression is: "When one door closes, another opens." It's hard to get him down—he bounces back like a rubber ball. He's the envy of his friends who wonder, how does he stay so upbeat?

The male Pig is his own worst enemy, sabotaging his best efforts at times. If he could get out of his own way, life would flow along without many major obstacles.

The male Pig is a jolly, lovable fellow who tends to gain weight as he ages. Despite his portly physique, women find his raw sensuality very seductive. He has a lusty sense of humor and an eye for the ladies. He is extremely gentle and never pushes himself on others, which is one of his many charms. Amazingly, even with his potbelly, gals naturally gravitate to his unaffected gentleness.

While he is jocular to the casual observer, anyone who is intimate with the male Pig knows that he has plenty of worries and concerns. These concerns stem from his innate perfectionism and insecurity. But everyone who knows him thinks he has nothing to worry about. The male Pig tells anyone who will listen that, "The ax is going to fall," but nobody believes it. Who could fire the fun-loving, hard-working Pig? Perhaps his insecurity stems from being duped one time too many. In any case, it makes him more cautious about getting into things too quickly. When he is overwhelmed, he takes solace in food, alcohol, or drugs. The stimulants give him the feeling of reassurance that all is right with the world—even if it isn't.

In the long run, the male Pig triumphs. He has long-range goals and a plan to make his dreams come true.

Despite his planning forward thinking, he isn't frugal—the male Pig never deprives himself of the fun things money can buy.

Because of his honesty and helpfulness, the male Pig is in great demand as a friend and a partner. The woman lucky enough to hook up with the him will not be disappointed. He makes a loyal husband, and his eternal optimism makes him a joy to be around.

LUCKY IN LOVE?

The lady Pig is shy and intimidated by the dating game. She dreams of being swept off her feet by a knight in shining armor. She may take a few wrong turns before she connects with that special guy, but her Cinderella fantasies keep her in good spirits until she finds him.

The lady Pig may be attracted to someone older than she is, because he's more likely to be already financially established. She's not interested in struggling through those early years living in a cramped space and driving an old, rusted car. She also needs money to start a family. Once she has settled down, she'll want to have kids right away. Her maternal time clock has been ticking, and she can't wait to dote on her little darlings.

The male Pig is passionate about many things, love in particular. He is extremely virile, and he has an enormous sexual appetite. Despite his intense sexuality, he's very shy when it comes to meeting the right partner; and he might need a shove in the right direction by a well-intentioned friend. The male Pig is looking for a long-lasting love with the person of his dreams. Still, he doesn't mind playing the field until he finds someone truly special. But he's not like the Dragon or the Horse, driven to put notches on his belt. He just wants to be king of his own domain.

Once he finds his true love, he gives his heart passionately and without reservation. Remember his vulnerabilities—you can easily hurt him without meaning to, and he won't bounce back quickly, the way a Tiger might. Once he settles down, he becomes the quintessential family man, taking his kids to the ballgame, coaching Little League, playing games, and even changing diapers.

FOR BETTER OR WORSE

Pig and Rat: The clever Rat and the industrious Pig make a terrific partnership for business and an amicable romantic pair. The Rat needs affection, which the Pig is willing to provide. In fact, this neediness on the Rat's part meshes perfectly with the Pig's desire to embrace others. Their initial passion will simmer down to a steady bubbling devotion. If this is you: You're both certain to be content in this pair.

Pig and Tiger: The Pig treasures the Tiger's passion, and the Tiger loves the Pig's popularity. They work like a well-oiled machine, putting ideas into motion and amassing a fortune, which they gladly share. The biggest problem this pair faces is not being able to say no or to slow down. The indulgence of the Pig and the zeal of the Tiger can work to their benefit or detriment. If this is you: You two have it made—so slow down and enjoy each other. You'll miss out on more than you bargain for if you don't commit to spending quality time together.

Pig and Rabbit: The arguments between these two optimists will be few and far between. They both strive for harmony, they both want world peace, and they are both flexible. Neither is driven to succeed and neither wants to be in the spotlight. This loving pair make excellent parents, and they will open their home to friends and strangers alike. If this is you: Everyone envies your peaceful coexistence. Enjoy the tranquility and each other.

Pig and Sheep: The Pig may be more indulgent than the Sheep, and the Sheep may be less focused than the Pig, but they both want the same thing: a solid, agreeable union. The flighty Sheep is kept on track by the more practical Pig, and together they can build a sizable bank account. They look forward to an empty nest so they can see the world. If this is you: You have a lot of fun together—at home and while traveling.

Pig and Rooster: The thick-skinned Pig isn't belittled by the Rooster, nor does the Pig get involved in the Rooster's bragging, which preserves the relationship. Pigs are masters of nonconfrontation and will say: "Yes, dear," and then do whatever they want. The Rooster appreciates the Pig's perseverance and wide circle of friends. If this is you: You two will prosper together.

Pig and Pig: Some people born under the same sign get along famously, like two Dogs. Two Pigs like to indulge, and they want the same things out of life; they have much in common. The problem comes when bad traits interfere with their smooth-flowing relationship. In the long run, Pigs tend to get on each other's nerves and need to rise above the pettiness to prosper as a couple. If this is you: Try not to sweat the small stuff—instead, focus on the big picture, which is a romantic and caring relationship.

Pig and Ox: Once again, the Ox dominates the union, which causes the good-natured Pig some discomfort. Both are honest and simple, which works to their favor. If the Ox can relax the rules a bit and allow the Pig some space, these two can make a go of it. If this is you: You two aren't the best or the worst of pairs—you're rather ho-hum.

Pig and Dragon: The flashy, impetuous Dragon may be too overbearing for the unobtrusive Pig, who prefers a quiet, ordered life. The Dragon has a giant ego and always needs to be right. While this doesn't bother the Pig, it does get to be a drag. Problems arise when the Pig begins to indulge and the Dragon frowns upon it. If there is an abundance of love and respect, these small glitches can be worked out. If this is you: Tolerance is the buzz-word that makes this union work. Find the middle road through compromise, and life will flow more smoothly.

Pig and Snake: The Snake is directly opposite the Pig in the Chinese zodiac, so it's no wonder that they don't see *eye to eye.* The Pig doesn't trust the secretive Snake and the Snake abhors the Pig's extravagances. Both are prone to negativity, which sends them into a downward spiral when they are together. If this is you: You both need to keep in mind that life is too short to be unhappy. But if you're really committed to making this relationship work, make sure you get outside help.

Pig and Horse: The Horse is quick—the Pig is less so. Yet these two can form a compatible union—perhaps without as much passion as with other pairings. If this is you: As long as the Horse can understand the passive nature of the Pig and the Pig doesn't try to rein the Horse in, you two can get along very well.

Pig and Monkey: The Monkey can run rings around the slow-moving Pig, and the Pig doesn't appreciate it. The Pig admires the clever Monkey, but the Monkey's trickery pricks the honest Pig's conscience. The Monkey doesn't like the Pig's spending habits, which can lead to trouble. If this is you: You've both got to learn to communicate openly about what your central priorities are. Once you do, you can decide whether compromising is an option or if you should go your separate ways.

Pig and Dog: The Pig wants to play, but the Dog wants to work. The Dog may find the Pig's jocular attitude annoying. The playful Pig may feel that the frugal Dog is too uptight. If this is you: With mutual respect and a common goal, you two can get along—but it will take hard work to make it happen.

WRITTEN IN THE STARS

Celebrity unions are fairly easy to analyze when we see them in terms of the Chinese zodiac. Since most people are familiar with the players, let's see if this political pair will sink or swim.

Hillary Rodham Clinton, junior senator from New York and former first lady, was born in Chicago on October 26, 1947, under the sign of the Pig. She attended prestigious Wellesley College and Yale University, where she earned a law degree. She is an intelligent, career-minded woman married to former president William Jefferson Clinton; and together they have one daughter, Chelsea. Bill Clinton was born in Hope, Arkansas, on August 19, 1946, under the sign of the Dog.

We can see that this is neither the best nor the worst pairing. Certainly Hillary has exhibited a laissez-faire attitude over Clinton's notorious dalliances—lady Pigs are peaceable by nature. Because of the innate differences between these two signs, they must put in the time and energy to make it work. However, the Dog is a sympathetic supporter of the Pig's ambitions and vice-versa.

Nevertheless, she is profoundly sensitive, a trait hidden by her ambitions as a politician. Apparently, they have found a happy medium and a common goal for they are still together, despite their roller coaster relationship for the past two decades.

A Final Word on the Chinese Zodiac

As you can see, the Chinese zodiac expresses the universe in a fixed order. When you sort your friends, parents, children, siblings, colleagues, lovers, potential mates, and your significant other into their respective astrological signs, you will get a better idea of how their innate personality traits cause them to interact with others—especially with you.

It should be noted that any of these signs have the potential to make a happy union. Some will take more work than others. If you're lucky, you will meet that special person and everything will flow without a hitch. Once you take into consideration that everyone has good traits as well as less desirable ones, it may be easier to accept that nobody is perfect. Yes, that means you, too! By accentuating the positive and trying to minimize the negative, we can all learn to coexist peaceably in our daily lives—even with those people who "rub us the wrong way."

From now on, observe people with these twelve animal signs in mind. For every characteristic that rubs you the wrong way, there might be at least one that you like. Take humans at face value, and try to see that their animal natures have a good deal to do with how they live their lives and how you live yours.

About the Author

L.A. Justice is a freelance photojournalist and author. She writes for numerous publications on a variety of subjects—from palmistry to herbal remedies. *What Women Really Want . . . and How They Can Get It* (Carroll & Graf, 2000) is her bestselling self-help book. She has written more than forty small guidebooks, which are sold in supermarkets across America, under the names L.A. Justice, Anne Liberty, LeAnne Wright, and Emily Lee. Currently, the mother of two grown daughters is writing, traveling, and taking photographs.